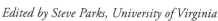

CCCC STUDIES IN WRITING & RHETORIC
Edited by Steve Parks, University of Virginia

The aim of the CCCC Studies in Writing & Rhetoric (SWR) Series is to influence how we think about language in action and especially how writing gets taught at the college level. The methods of studies vary from the critical to historical to linguistic to ethnographic, and their authors draw on work in various fields that inform composition—including rhetoric, communication, education, discourse analysis, psychology, cultural studies, and literature. Their focuses are similarly diverse— ranging from individual writers and teachers, to work on classrooms and communities and curricula, to analyses of the social, political, and material contexts of writing and its teaching.

SWR was one of the first scholarly book series to focus on the teaching of writing. It was established in 1980 by the Conference on College Composition and Communication (CCCC) in order to promote research in the emerging field of writing studies. As our field has grown, the research sponsored by SWR has continued to articulate the commitment of CCCC to supporting the work of writing teachers as reflective practitioners and intellectuals.

We are eager to identify influential work in writing and rhetoric as it emerges. We thus ask authors to send us project proposals that clearly situate their work in the field and show how they aim to redirect our ongoing conversations about writing and its teaching. Proposals should include an overview of the project, a brief annotated table of contents, and a sample chapter. They should not exceed 10,000 words.

To submit a proposal, please register as an author at www.editorial manager.com/nctebp. Once registered, follow the steps to submit a proposal (be sure to choose SWR Book Proposal from the drop-down list of article submission types).

T0262600

Queer Techné

Bodies, Rhetorics, and Desire
in the History of Computing

Patricia Fancher
University of California, Santa Barbara

Conference on College
Composition and
Communication

National Council of
Teachers of English

National Council of Teachers of English
340 N. Neil St., Suite #104, Champaign, Illinois 61820
www.ncte.org

Staff Editor: Cynthia Gomez
Manuscript Editor: Bonny Graham
Series Editor: Steve Parks
Interior Design: Mary Rohrer
Cover Design: Pat Mayer
Cover Images: iStock: mammuth and Galina Kamenskaya

ISBN 978-0-8141-0173-5 (paperback); ISBN 978-0-8141-0174-2 (ebook);
ISBN 978-0-8141-0175-9 (PDF)

It is the policy of NCTE in its journals and other publications to provide a forum for the open discussion of ideas concerning the content and the teaching of English and the language arts. Publicity accorded to any particular point of view does not imply endorsement by the Executive Committee, the Board of Directors, or the membership at large, except in announcements of policy, where such endorsement is clearly specified.

NCTE provides equal employment opportunity (EEO) to all staff members and applicants for employment without regard to race, color, religion, sex, national origin, age, physical, mental or perceived handicap/disability, sexual orientation including gender identity or expression, ancestry, genetic information, marital status, military status, unfavorable discharge from military service, pregnancy, citizenship status, personal appearance, matriculation or political affiliation, or any other protected status under applicable federal, state, and local laws.

Every effort has been made to provide current URLs and email addresses, but because of the rapidly changing nature of the web, some sites and addresses may no longer be accessible.

Library of Congress Control Number: 2023950913

CONTENTS

ACKNOWLEDGMENTS

I STARTED THIS PROJECT AS A GRADUATE student, and I was curious about Alan Turing. I wanted to pull on that thread of curiosity so that I could weave queerness, gender, and emotion into the history of computing. As I did so, I found Turing's community of queer friends and collaborators. I found this community through no small amount of digging, researching, and a touch of imagination. My own research process has been similarly supported by a larger community of friends, mentors, collaborators, and editors. I hope this acknowledgment holds up a fuller picture of the intellectual and social community out of which this book was developed. Here are just a few of the threads that held me together through my research and writing process.

I am indebted to my dissertation committee members at Clemson University, Steven B. Katz, Cynthia Haynes, D. Travers Scott, and Diane Perpich. They each enriched my thinking and supported me in my first serious research endeavor. My committee's support and training in queer feminist methodologies have forever inspired my research.

That dissertation would never have grown into a book if it had not been for the enthusiasm and support of Steven Parks, editor of the Studies in Writing & Rhetoric Series. He is a real advocate for burgeoning voices in the study of rhetoric and composition. He has a talent for asking the exact question that I most needed to answer, though I hadn't seen it myself. I'm grateful for the entire editorial staff at the National Council of Teachers of English. Bonny Graham devoted her talents through attentive editing that improved both my clarity and style. Kurt Austin, Cynthia Gomez, and Emmy Gilbert shepherded my book through the publication process, keeping me on track and encouraging me along the way.

This book would not be possible without the archival materials held in the History of Computing Collection at the University of Manchester Library. In 2019, the staff welcomed me into their spaces, offered support, and directed me to the best spots for coffee in Manchester. I also depended on digital resources held at University of Manchester Library, Turing Digital Archive held at King's College Cambridge, and the Computer History Museum in California. I am grateful to the imaging staff and archivists for supporting me by digitizing materials, answering questions, and sharing their extensive expertise on the history of computing. My archival research travel was funded by a grant from the Agnodike Travel Research Fellowship for the Commission on Women and Gender in History of Science, Technology and Medicine. My travel was also supported by the Non-Senate Faculty Grant secured by the UC-AFT Union and the University of California, Santa Barbara.

After I secured an advance contract for this book, the world shut down in response to COVID. Most of this book was written in fits and spurts stolen from the innumerable changing demands on my time to meet the needs of my students and my family. I am deeply grateful to Charles Bazerman for his support through the Bazerman Faculty Fellowship at UCSB, which bought me the time to focus on completing a final manuscript. I don't know how I could have finished this book without Charles and the gift of time that the Bazerman Faculty Fellowship provided. I enjoyed the encouragement and support of the entire Writing Program at UC Santa Barbara, especially the leadership, Linda Adler-Kassner, Karen Lunsford, and Amy Propen. On a day-to-day basis, the women in UCSB's Write-On-Site community offered me support, encouragement, and accountability. They also simply believed that I could write a book and that I should write a book, and their confidence in me lifted me when I needed it most.

I am deeply grateful for my chosen family. We aren't held together by blood, contracts, or any traditional family structure. We are held together by choice. We choose each other. I am thankful every day to be chosen by such intelligent, caring, funny, loving people. Most of my family has never read a page of this book in progress. I still could not have done it without y'all: D. Inés Casillas, Caitlin Gorman, Per Hoel, Carlyn Sander, Eve Sanford, Martha Sprigge, Luz Lorenzana Twigg, Ellen O'Connell Whittet, Talia White, and Alison Williams. In particular, Caitlin listened to me stress out about what "queer" even means. Ellen walked miles with me talking about books we've read and books we're writing. Luz showed up and reminded me that queer joy is a resource on which I thrive. But I should stop gushing about my friends. You have a book to read. To end, I thank you, sweet reader, for your attention and your generosity.

1

Queer Techné

IN 1948, THE MANCHESTER MARK I WAS HARD at work in the University of Manchester Computing Lab in Manchester, England, as one of the world's earliest stored-program computers. This computer (see Figure 1) would hardly be recognized as a computer by today's standards. It stored memory on a cathode-ray tube, which could program up to 1,024 bits. Billions operate in our phones now. Wires hung overhead. It was programmed with switches, nodes, and levers and required operators to run up and down flights of stairs. The women who operated this machine remarked on the physical strain required to program and operate the Mark I. It did not yet have anything that we would recognize as an operating system. Instead, it included a printer that allowed data to be written on and read from paper tape.

The History of Computing Collection at the University of Manchester Archives includes documentation of the development of England's early computing efforts, starting with the Manchester Mark I and the subsequent model, the Ferranti Mark I, the first fully programmable commercial computer in operation by 1950. As I searched these archival holdings, I was struck by how often the technical writing that documented the development of early computers veered into the personal and emotional. "Machines take me by surprise with great frequency," said Alan Turing in 1950. And he was not alone in this feeling of surprise. The University of Manchester computing logbook documenting the daily use of Mark I includes the operators' experiences (see Figure 2):

Figure 1: Manchester Mark I computer circa 1948. Photograph created in 2022 by compiling all existing photos of the Mark I to create a highly detailed panoramic of the computer.

"Clodding intolerable, I quit!" in 1951.
"Disaster!" in 1952.
"Machine quite good on the whole," in 1953.
"Machine working like a lamb," in 1958.
Until in red ink and all caps the logbook reads, "Smelled smoke in the mercury room. . . .
Switched off rest of machine."
"THE END OF MARK I—R.I.P.
REMOVED IN JUNE 1959 FOR BURIAL"

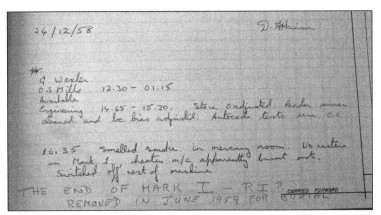

Figure 2: Manchester Mark I engineer's log, December 24, 1958.

In this book, I explore the history of digital computing not through the technical components of the machine itself but through experiences like the ones quoted above. I offer an intimate narrative connected to the bodies, desires, and relationships of men, women, and machines. To construct this intimate narrative, I introduce *queer techné* as a process driven by desire, play, and risk. Queer techné was a vital resource for technological innovation in the archival materials of the history of digital computing. I define *queer techné* by focusing first on Alan Turing. I then broaden my scope so that the network of queer computing encompasses more relationships, embodied experiences, communities, and tensions among those communities.

I explore the queer techné of digital computing in the archives of the University of Manchester Computing Lab held in the British History of Computing Collection. This archival resource is unique because it documents one of the earliest and most innovative digital computers. Most famously, this was the lab in which Alan Turing worked. Alan Turing is credited as a founding father of digital computing. He was also gay and persecuted for his sexuality, which he refused to hide. It is common to imagine Turing as an isolated hero—books and movies have portrayed him as such. In 2014, I watched the popular Turing biopic *Imitation Game* portray him as a recluse—his queerness forcing him into a closet that separated him from the world, with only his computer as a friend—and I questioned the purpose of this isolation narrative. Who did it serve? And how accurate could it be? The Turing archives offer rich evidence that Turing was not alone. He was neither friendless nor loveless. Queer folks know how to find our people and build communities.

I extend the analysis of queer techné by tracing the queer community that collaborated with Alan Turing toward early computer science and programming. Using archival evidence to uncover the queer embodied practices of these men, I argue that these queer embodied friendships are epistemically significant for early digital computing, especially in experiments toward the possibility of intelligent machines.

Next, I expand to a broader context that includes women who were computer operators and programmers. From this analysis, I locate tensions of inclusion and exclusion among marginalized communities. Hired as assistants, these women earned advanced degrees and then went on to be internationally regarded as experts in computing. But they have been largely unrecognized in the history of digital computers until recently.

These communities overlapped but never integrated, nor were they mutually supportive. This tension is important to examine. I show how the queer men were able to embrace joy and play. They created intellectual and personal connections within a homophobic society. However, the fourth chapter reminds us that even marginalized communities can actively push out other marginalized communities. To be specific, the gay men excluded and dismissed the women they worked alongside in the University of Manchester Computing Lab. The joyful and playful intellectual work that the queer men were able to enjoy was unequally distributed. Chapter 4 offers a feminist counterbalance by integrating women's contributions and embodied techné into this larger narrative. These communities occupied the same spaces and did very similar work; however, their embodied techné differed as significantly as their experiences in the world.

This book is an initial exploration into the queer techné of one particular community and of one particular computing lab in the 1940s and 1950s. In the archives that are largely technical, I searched for the embodied, emotional, and affectionate. Even in discourse communities and genres that were committed to efficiency, I easily found playfulness. By introducing queer techné, I also invite readers to consider the queer experiences behind computing. I introduce the first model of computer-generated writing and locate its queer longing. I hope this inspires others to approach ChatGPT and similar forms of AI-generated writing with an ear for queer techné. What could its queer potential be? Its capacity for queer desire? And what boundaries upon that desire are most immutable? How can my own queer longing be explored through AI-based interactions? I invite readers to consider the queer crafting that may lie beneath the surface of other technologies, including early AI writing as well as emerging AI writing technologies.

I am reminded of Eve Sedgwick's words from *Epistemology of the Closet*: "An understanding of virtually any aspect of modern Western culture must be, not merely incomplete, but damaged in its central substance to the degree that it does not incorporate a critical analysis of modern homo/heterosexual definition" (1). Her words gave me permission so many years ago when I was a graduate student with a hunch that there was a story worth exploring in the queer history of computers. Her words remind me that my own queer experience informs my own research project. As such, I have tried to integrate narratives of my own queer techné through each chapter to situate this research in relation to my personal experiences. I invite others to attune themselves to the queer techné that enlivens other technologies, crafts, and practices. To set up my analysis of queer techné, I first define my three anchor terms: *techné*, *embodiment*, and *queer*.

DEFINING *TECHNÉ*

Techné is learning by doing. It is knowing through practice. I cannot practice techné exclusively by studying a textbook, learning the parts, or memorizing definitions. I practice music by playing instruments. I practice writing by keeping my hands to a keyboard. Knitting is learned with needles in hands. Techné is the work of learning a craft by crafting. It also requires knowledge of the rules, theories, and physical practice. While rules may be applied, techné involves both theoretical knowledge and experience to allow for "a cunning set of flexible strategies that partially control . . . human or natural events" (Schryer et al. 239).

Contemporary scholars of techné have emphasized the importance of embodiment for this mode of invention and knowledge production.[1] Kelly Pender emphasizes that the concept of "craft" or "art" focuses too narrowly on the work done, but techné includes the rich connections between knowledge, experience, and trained practice that all together are key for productive arts. A criterion for techné is that it "locates its end outside the process of making in the use of the thing made" (Pender 5). For computing, the techné would be the embodied experience and knowledge of its inventors and operators. But so often the techné of computing is overlooked for the study of the machine, the thing made. This connection between knowing, doing, and producing is also key to understanding the complexity of techné (Atwill and Lauer; Wickman; Edwell et al.). Together, embodied practice and knowledge produce both art and phronesis, or practical wisdom (Kosma and Buchanan).

When we focus on the embodiment of techné, we also shift to include the social work of invention. In "Race, Rhetoric, and Technology," Angela Haas critiques contemporary analysis of technology that isolates the tool, which can seem to make the object stand alone outside of cultural and historical contexts. Instead, she asks us to define technologies as techné: social and technical processes that are always embodied in social, material contexts. This shift allows her to take up the study of technology with a decolonial methodology. Techné as a practice becomes a decolonial methodology that resists the tendency to study new or emerging technology and resists the colonial hierarchies that exclude the advanced technologies of Native communities. An example of this is her analysis of the wampum, a beaded belt that "embodies memory" ("Wampum" 80). Wampum belts function as hypertext across communities and times, "signifying a surviving intellectual tradition that communicates living stories of a living culture" (92). Although the context and the purpose of her work differ from mine, Haas's work on Indigenous techné is vital for my research because I follow her shift from a tool to a process. She also places the process of techné within communities. From Haas's work, I ground techné in embodied practices as well as in the communities, the collaborations, and the values of those communities.

Following Haas's argument to shift from studying technology to studying techné, I focus not on the computer as an object or tool but rather on computing as a practice requiring theoretical expertise and embodied practice. Therefore, when I identify techné in this book, I identify verbs: actions from which knowledge is composed. However, techné is not rote action or habit but rather practiced, thoughtful craft toward productive ends. In this way, computers are not techné. Computers are the end product. In Turing's day, computing included practices such as calculating data and programming machines to write love letters as well as develop nuclear weapons. Computing, the process, is techné.

I consistently use the term *computing* instead of *computers*. I do this for a few reasons. First, the verb form shifts the focus from the tool as a stand-alone object to the process of doing computing work with a variety of different machines. For instance, a particular computer may complete a task, but it does so only through the labor of people, the support of infrastructure, and the accumulated syntax of programming languages. Computing refers to the social, embodied technical process of invention, development, programming, and completion of computing tasks.

Defining techné as a social process also includes a broader range of people and kinds of work involved in computing. I expand beyond those who are most often given the title of inventor to include a wider community that sustained and labored toward the development and operation of computing machines. The social process of techné also foregrounds connections among people, thereby shifting from an individualistic notion of invention to a collaborative, community-based model. I am also able to broaden the scope of the project so that the work of women stands as a predecessor to the computing machines. Computing was women's work. Women were computers. In postwar Manchester, women such as Cicely Popplewell and Audrey Bates, who had gained computing experience during World War II, earned master's degrees in mathematics. Most often, they are identified as assistants; however, archival materials demonstrate that they were the primary operators, gatekeepers, and programmers for these early computers. Popplewell rewrote Turing's programming manual—the first version was unusable—and her version became a standard document. In addition, her primary contribution to computing was through writing, especially writing programming instructions for the Mark I.

When I write about computing, I include the margins of technical invention. Cecilia Shelton introduces the concept of the techné of marginality:

> When marginalized people navigate systems not designed for their inclusion, they not only apply this critical marginality to the labor that is required to circumvent, subvert, renegotiate the systems for their own survival and success, but they also leave the specialized communication and navigation infrastructures (i.e., technical communication) in place to sustain the labor moving forward. (19)

Shelton's techné of marginality resonates with my project by recognizing the importance of looking toward marginalized communities, the labor that often sustains community, the resistance to assimilation, and the embrace of the "margins as [a] rich & powerful site" of resistance and community connection (Shelton 107). I find similar patterns in queer communities in the archives of digital computing. However, I hesitate to find too close a parallel between Shelton's work on Black women's experiences and the lived experiences of white women and queer men in my research. Shelton specifically identifies rhetorical practices that resist the patriarchal, colonial influence of the Western rhetorical tradition. Early computer operators and programmers were not just marginal; they were also oppressed oppressors. As such, they simultaneously experienced being pushed to the margins while also actively and intentionally marginalizing others, including Black women. Alan Turing disrespected and disregarded the women who worked in the University of Manchester Computing Lab. In turn, women did nothing to protect Turing, nor did they continue to collaborate with him when he was outed, tried, and punished for homosexuality. All these people and the overall project of computing supported colonial logics and the British Empire. Therefore, their position in the margins is complicated by their privileged position in relation to white supremacy and colonialism. Each chapter identifies these communities as oppressed oppressors, both in the ways their marginality was a rich resource for knowledge production and in the ways this was used to perpetuate colonial systems.

DEFINING *EMBODIMENT*

Embodiment is a key term in this book, as theories of embodiment are central to theories of both techné and queerness. Like the other terms, embodiment lends itself to actions. In *Volatile Bodies*, feminist philosopher Elizabeth Grosz argues that theories of The Body too often assume a stable, singular theory of human materiality. There is no singular body but rather a diversity of bodies. If a body is theorized as stable, singular, and established, that theory removes bodies from temporality and movement. But bodies change, grow, age, move, break, heal, connect, assemble, and share. To focus on the movement and temporal significance of our bodies, theories of embodiment ask us to think of bodies as always moving, processing, and changing.

Feminist philosophers of technology Donna Haraway (*Simians*) and Katherine Hayles both theorize embodiment in relation to and co-constituted through technologies. These feminist scholars of technology are attuned to embodiment as a process that, in social contexts, allows particular bodies to resist, twist, and alter bodily codes. As Hayles writes, "Formed by technology at the same time that [embodied practices] create technology, embodiment mediates between technology and discourse by creating new experiential frameworks that serve as boundary markers for the creation of corresponding discursive systems" (205). The woman as a computer is an example of Hayles's point: Computing is formed by these women's embodied practices. At the same time, the invention of digital computing, the gendering of this labor, and the changing demands of computing also formed definitions of who was an expert in computing and why.

Within rhetoric and composition, we have widely accepted and theorized the relationships between embodiment and rhetoric. There was a moment in which we collectively had to remind scholars that bodies matter, documented best in the collection *Rhetorical Bodies* edited by Jack Selzer and Sharon Crowley. Now, *embodiment* is a key term, especially in feminist rhetoric (Booher and Jung; Schell and Rawson; Johnson et al.), technical communication (Melonçon, "Toward"; Moore and Richards; Fountain; Haas and Witte), cultural rhetoric (Bratta and Powell; Cedillo and Bratta;

Cobos et al.), and composition studies (Crowley; Fleckenstein; Arola and Wysocki; Janine Butler; Cedillo, "Diversity" and "What Does It Mean").

In the collection of feminist rhetoric key terms published in *Peitho*, Maureen Johnson et al. situate embodiment for feminist rhetoricians: "To think about rhetoric, we must think about bodies" (39). This collaboratively written concept statement demarcates embodiment as a specifically feminist key term that is also a central theory for rhetoric broadly. Similarly, Jay Dolmage argues that, even in its long history, "rhetoric has a body—has bodies" ("Metis" 22). The embodiment of rhetoric includes both discourse about bodies as well as the rhetorical potency of bodies themselves. On the one hand, our discourses about bodies compose our knowledge, shape our experience, and define how we know bodies. On the other hand, our bodies and embodied experiences constitute our discourses, give life and energy to our words, and shape our knowledge.

Indigenous rhetorics are vital to include in any discussion of embodied rhetoric because they weave together relationships between diverse bodies. For Malea Powell, Indigenous rhetorics outline an ethical model that centers accountability toward "all our relations." These relations include a rich array of embodied connections between community and the living world, animals, plants, humans, our land, and lives (Bratta and Powell). Gabriela Raquel Ríos stresses that these relations are not metaphors in the way that some scholars will theorize ecologies as metaphors ("Cultivating") or spatial and border metaphors ("Performing") as abstract theories with few connections to material, lived experience. Instead, Indigenous scholars account for these relations between people, land, and community in literal, concrete ways. As Ríos defines *relationality*, "Indigenous relationality recognizes that humans and the environment are in a relationship that is co-constituted and not just interdependent. Additionally, Indigenous relationality recognizes the environment's capacity to produce relations" ("Cultivating" 63).

While embodiment has long been theorized in rhetoric, in 2013, Lisa Meloncon found that there was insufficient scholarship on embodiment in technical and professional communication. She identified embodiment theorized in only two sources in the discipline: Christina Haas and Stephen P. Witte in 2001 and Beverly Sauer in 2002. Building on these sources, Melonçon outlined intersections between theories of embodiment and technical communication, offering a necessary connection: "In the everydayness of technical communication, its usefulness rests in foregrounding the necessity to proceed with caution, to actually consider the myriad of ethical dimensions embedded in every technology embodiment" ("Toward" 76). Embodiment is significant for technical and professional writing because it focuses on the everydayness of technical work and because of these immediate ethical implications for our technical writing.

Building on Melonçon, scholars of technical communication have taken up this line of research to include embodiment as epistemic (Fountain; Edwell et al.), embodiment and technologies (Jack, "Leviathan"; Melonçon, "Bringing" and "Embodied"), and enacting social justice through technical communication research (Jones et al.; Rose and Walton; Walton and Agboka). Taken together, this emerging site of research on embodiment in technical communication shares a claim with rhetoric of bodies that embodiment is epistemic. That claim is of critical importance because embodied experience, through practice, is epistemic. It means that engineers, designers, and technical communicators ground their knowledge, expertise, and rhetorical strategies in embodied experiences. Technical communication, in its everyday messiness, is a rich site of embodied rhetoric because it documents the challenges, processes, and physical experiences of struggling and succeeding.

These theories refuse to separate mind and body, experience and knowledge. Scholars of technology, especially Safiya Umoja Noble, have extensively documented the ways that sexism and racism continue to be encoded into new computing technologies. The embodiment of the community, currently white, straight men, is the techné that dominates computing technologies. I ask: Could it be otherwise? Might queer embodiments cultivate a different techné? Could they approach technologies in nonnormative ways?

DEFINING *QUEER*

The term *queer* has had a promiscuous history. It has been used and applied broadly, with flexibility and eagerness. But this promiscuity does not mean the term lacks definition. It can seem to have too much flexibility, such that it lacks specificity. However, I offer that queer theorists are invested in exploring and progressing definitions of what queer is and could be. The definition of *queer* changes because we need it to do so much. In their introduction to the *Routledge Handbook of Queer Rhetoric,* Jacqueline Rhodes and Jonathan Alexander also reflect on the expansive definition of *queer* that appears in the large, diverse collection. Because of this, they resist defining *queer rhetoric* neatly. Instead, they write:

> Queer rhetoric now, provisionally, might mean thinking and writing about bodies, intimacies, pleasures, identities, communities, practices, activisms, and politics in challenging and often contrary ways. That's not to say that "queer" and "contrary" are interchangeable. They're not. But it is to say that queer remains for many writers a modality of resistance (but not just negatively so). Queer is not just saying no. It is also saying yes, and affirming and validating to different ways of being in the world, perhaps to being in the world differently. But not always and not in every way. (1)

This definition applies to my own use of *queer* in this book. In particular, I want to emphasize that queering can be both resistance and saying "no, I prefer not." In addition, queering invites us to say yes, to desire, to ways of being, to play, and to joy. In "Queer: An Impossible Subject for Composition," Alexander and Rhodes suggest that queer rhetoric reaches toward the impossible limits as a field of research because it challenges the boundaries of academic knowledge making. And they cherish that impossibility, writing: "We embrace and fail to embrace the excess of such a queer[ed/ing] knowing" (177).

Like *techné* and *embodiment,* I prefer to let *queer* be a verb: *queering.* Queering is antinormative but not randomly. To queer is also to embrace desire, longing, and pleasure, to hold on to that embrace well beyond socially acceptable norms. From those practices queer techné emerges, which locates queer desire and play in everyday habits and life.

One of the earliest definitions of queer rhetorics comes from Margaret Morrison's *Pre/Text* essay. She opens with a celebration of the instability that comes with queer identity, making stable definitions of gender and sexuality laughable. Instead, desire and embodiment enliven queer rhetorics. She defines queer rhetoric as "desire/bodies [that] put into play a kind of linguistic music that so confuses the Symbolic's binary-based systems that we are forced to begin to think differently" (13). Queer rhetorics are resistant to normativity and driven by bodies, desire. Jean Bessette adds an important nuance to this definition: while queerness is antinormative, thereby suggesting *queer* is antithetical to definition, queer rhetorics are not ahistorical nor without definition because rhetorics are always in situ, located in a community, place, and historical moment ("Queer Rhetoric"). Bessette productively pairs *queer* and *rhetorics* so that queerness is defined in relation to the normative practices in specific contexts.

I define *queerness* much as I have defined *techné*: the end product does not define what is queer. Queering is an action, and we locate it by its use, experience, and process. Queer is not the stable identity category; it is the path of getting out of heteronormativity. It is the movements that prompt new questions. This focuses on queer as lived experience. I also argue that gender, sex, and identity are not abstract identity categories, nor are any of these identities stable. Gender and sexual identity are formed both through points of stability as well as through change and incongruity. I am especially drawn to the definition of *queer* by essayist Harron Walker in her reflection on sexual identity:

A life is better understood through an individual's actions over their labels, their verbs over their nouns. It's like what Dusty Springfield once said when asked about her sexuality. "I know I'm perfectly capable of being swayed by a girl as by a boy," she told the *London Evening Standard* in 1970. She didn't say who she was, but she said who she did, and isn't that what matters in the end? It's a lot hotter, anyway.

Her last line, "It's a lot hotter," sounds flippant, but I think it is central to the definition of *queer*. I hope that by locating the action and process of queering, I can also continue to foreground the embodiments, the physical reality and lived experience, of queer people and communities. Eric Darnell Pritchard has taught us that queer Black communities must be understood in both material and discursive ways, including fashion and movement. By emphasizing doing, Pritchard attunes us to rhetorics that are generative, caring, and loving.

Queering is tied to desire, pleasure, and blowing up the multitude of ways that people experience desire. Queer theory could feel hot, I hope. It should at least feel hotter than clicking a box on a form. Queering feels more exciting than adding a flag to my Twitter profile or my office door. I may do these things as a signal for students. But queerness is not as simple as claiming a category, and I hope it is a lot more fun than that as well. Personally, queering is what I do when I build a life full of partnerships, pleasures, and families that look and feel different, that look and feel in ways that make us question what counts as partnership, pleasure, or family. My lived experience is my queerness. My lived experience motivates how I define *queer techné* and why I care.

QUEER TECHNÉ

I define *queer techné* in order to build on previous work of queer rhetorics with a focus on the practice and craft of being queer and the knowledge produced by these queer practices. Queer techné is attuned to the craft of desire, the art of capacious wanting, and the practices of pleasure, especially the desires that resist heteronormative constraints. Queer techné recognizes the practices of these desires and celebrates them as resources for invention.

Queer techné was first suggested in *Techné: Queer Meditations on Writing the Self* by Jacqueline Rhodes and Jonathan Alexander. Their definition begins, "We pose the techné of queer sexuality as a sort of generative lived knowledge; it is a view of techné that points less to the prescriptive how-to sense of the term and more to the ethical, civic dimension" (116). This creative, academic text theorizes queer techné through personal, archival, performative, and multimodal digital design. Here, Rhodes and Alexander perform a generative process of becoming—becoming queerly—in the world as well as in their own compositional processes. Each time I return to this multimodal scholarly text, I am touched. Rhodes offers us hands and earth, which remind us of our roots, both our families and the feminist roots on which Rhodes built her life. Alexander explores his family's personal archive, which offers us a view into queer Southern life. He explores these archives as well as his own desire to feel closer to his family. The design of this text performs queer rhetoric by presenting us with bodies, texts, and media that blur boundaries between academic, personal, erotic, intellectual, and political discourses. Each section is designed slightly differently, with different colors, layouts, text styles, etc., featuring the multiplicity of queer aesthetics as well as queer experience.

A more recent discussion related to queer techné can be found in Michael Faris's "Sex Education Comics: Feminist and Queer Approaches to Alternative Sex Education." Faris theorizes "towards a sexual techné," which he defines as both technical and deeply relational. "This sexual literacy and agency becomes a sort of techné, a contextual practice that is both individual (related to identity and one's own sexual interests and desires) and shared" (106). Relational practices of consent are central to Faris's sexual techné, which connect individual desire with shared ethics. Sexual techné integrates a civic component that centers our responsibilities and relations to others. He further explains that this sexual techné is a "relational and embodied practice—an ethic of both self and relationality. That is, it is not reducible to simply skill or technical knowledge, but is rather generative of new relationships and ways of being in the world" (109).

It is worth reflecting on a tension that arises when pairing *queer* and *techné*. Techné is associated with productivity, utility. Queerness has been theorized as resistant to utility, intentionally inefficient and unproductive. Are these terms not at odds? I find this tension exciting. Queer techné invites us to think about processes and crafts outside of their end product. It asks us to consider art, process, and the experience of making as valuable before and beyond their production value.

Queer techné is also attuned to capacious desires, wanting more and longing toward a world of collective possibility. As I theorize queer techné and locate it in early computer archives, I insist on centering desire and joy, as I have learned from queer Black feminist scholars, especially Audre Lorde. In "Uses of the Erotic," Lorde highlights the erotic as a path toward a rich life:

> The aim of each thing which we do is to make our lives and the lives of our children richer and more possible. Within the celebration of the erotic in all our endeavors, my work becomes a conscious decision—a longed-for bed which I enter gratefully and from which I rise up empowered. (31)

I further hear the joy of queer erotics resonating in "Poetry Is Not a Luxury," as Lorde meditates on art and beauty as vital resources for social movements to channel experience into word and action. I am grateful for the generations of Black feminists whose work is committed to both critique and care, with nuance for the politics and necessity of pleasure and joy. bell hooks challenges me anew each time I teach her thinking on eros and erotics, which is not reducible to sexual desire, to imagine how we can teach in such a way that "love is bound to flourish" ("Eros" 62). More recently, I am indebted to adrienne maree brown's *Pleasure Activism* for reminding us that, as activists, resistance is only sustainable if we also invest in joy, play, pleasure, and communities of care.

Within the University of Manchester Computing Lab, the community of queer men collaborated on experiments and playful writing. While the broader history of computing is committed to utility and expedience, in this small community, we find queer alternatives that explore computing for the sake of computing. Turing dreamt of a computer that could pass: pass as human and also pass as a woman. His closest friend, Robin Gandy, writes first to ask for advice on his dissertation about mathematics and logic but dedicates much of the letter to updates on a full slate of potential romantic partners. Christopher Strachey programmed a computer to write love letters and posted them throughout the halls of the University of Manchester Computing Lab. This was a group of queer friends who worked together and worked queerly to imagine futures for computational thinking. Their joy and pleasure in their creative intellectual work animate both their technical writing and their personal letters. Still, the queer techné I identify is not the norm, nor the dominant mode in the history of computing. Turing's and Strachey's writing are outliers, which is no surprise. Scholar of queer writing Stacey Waite reflects,

> Writing queer is possible in the most momentary and fleeting ways, but it is imperative—for queer scholars especially but perhaps for all scholars of writing—to resist the writing norms and assumptions that inform how we compose, to try to cup in our hands, however briefly and however impossibly, whatever water we can hold long enough for a small drink. (48)

In this queer counternarrative of the history of computing, I pull on strands, hope they hold, and pray that I can weave them into a satisfying account of the play and pleasure of queer techné. There are going to be gaps and tears. Stories are stretched thin. That is our queer rhetorical legacy.

This imaginative, propositional work in the queer history and future of computing has already begun. Notably, in 1991 Jack Halberstam imagined in "Automating Gender: Postmodern Feminisms in the Age of the Intelligent Machine" the potential for feminism to find positive and productive uses for theories of artificial intelligence. AI asks us to question the distinction between human and machine, intelligence and mechanics. By extension, intelligence, gender, and humanity all become unstable categories. Halberstam identifies this first and foremost with Turing:

> Turing's experience of gender instability [during chemical castration as a punishment for being convicted of "gross

indecency"] suggests that the body may in fact be, both materially and libidinally, a product of technology inasmuch as injections of hormones can transform it from male to female; second, desire provides the random element necessary to a technology's definition as intelligent. In other words, the body may be scientifically altered in order to force "correct" gender identification, but desire remains as interference running across a binary technologic. (143–44)

I build on these arguments about Turing, gender, and ways of knowing by locating the queer techné of digital computing. As Halberstam points out, feminism and queer theory both benefit from tracing the desires, materially and libidinally, that we find in the history of computing.

Kara Keeling recognizes the racist and heteronormative logics that have historically been built (see also McPherson) into computer operating systems. At the same time, she looks forward, imagining and theorizing a possible queer operating system that "insists upon forging and facilitating uncommon, irrational, imaginative, and/or unpredictable relationships between and among what currently are perceptible as living beings and the environment in the interest of creating value(s) that facilitate just relations" (154). Her imagined Queer OS also operates through failure, including "malfunction within technologies that secure 'robot' and 'human,' a malfunction with a capacity to reorder things . . . and make what was legible soar into unpredictable relations" (157). This theme of failure by any measure, but certainly by measures of efficiency, will be especially pronounced in the early experimental computing work in the University of Manchester Computing Lab. At the same time, a queer computing framework is not pure imagination. Jess Tran and Elizabeth Patitsas identify queer artifacts that together map a "faint terrain of queer CS" (15). Faint though it may be, they create ways that users can exploit design failures to queerly appropriate even the most normative of platforms like Facebook.

Queer techné invites us to think capaciously about sexuality and technology. Queer techné invites us to consider desire, pleasure, and affect as central to our work of making and being made. Pleasure and desire are the point of the process. Queer techné may be the process by which we enact what José Esteban Muñoz would call queer world building. Queer techné may be one means of making Muñoz's queer utopia into a path by which to "enact new and better pleasures, other ways of being in the world, and ultimately new worlds" (1).

COLONIAL LEGACIES OF COMPUTING

While we dream and theorize toward ever more queer futures, we continue to live and build knowledge within political and historical contexts. Jean Bessette traces how the meaning and power of queer rhetoric emerges within existing power structures ("Queer Rhetoric"). While I look for the potential of queer techné in the history of computing, queer techné exists within colonial power structures. Therefore, these archival sources I analyze are inextricable from the context in which British colonial logics were reinvented in economic, social, and technical structures, including computers. British computing was only possible through the needs, support, and funding of British colonial power, and the drive to develop computers was fueled by that power.

Accounting for queer techné and its embodied performance also means locating those queer embodiments in broader social, political contexts. To what extent does the marginality of queerness resist dominant political structures? On the other hand, how might class, race, and gender privilege support queerness? To what extent has queerness become co-opted for colonial, racist power? If I were to focus only on the embodied experiences and practices of early computer operators, I may focus so closely on women and their experiences that I might fail to place their embodied experiences in a broader context. Similarly, I realize that I am easily charmed by all things queer. Yet, queer does not exist in a vacuum.

Embodiments, subjectivities, and technologies all intertwine in politics and culture. The model of British governance is so closely tied to the model of computer technology that historian of science and technology Jon Agar asserts, "to study the history of technology is to study the state, and vice versa" (3). Foucault writes that biopower, as opposed to sovereign power, "gave rise as well to comprehensive measures, statistical assessments, and interventions aimed at the entire social body or at groups taken as a whole" (*History* 146). And the computer is a vital tool enabling this biopower. Although Foucault does not discuss computing technologies specifically, Agar writes the history of computers as the central tool for the British government bureaucracy to regulate global populations. He explains that the government was metaphorically, in its ideal scenario, functioning like a machine: efficient, unbiased, based on general processes that are applied to a range of different tasks. There was a debate over how to manage India and other colonies. Who should make decisions about local colonies, the local civil servants or centralized police?

Led by the technocratic class centered in London, a shift away from local authority toward centralized governance was made. Agar explains,

> The pragmatist model of imperial authority was the local human administrator, who, although trained at college in Britain, embodied skills and knowledge of governance gained through experience. The technocrats, on the other hand, were confident that the stability of statistics meant that power could be centralized: on the basis of statistics someone in London, say, could reliably guide policy in the imperial periphery. (106)

Mechanical ideology for governance was extended to include greater surveillance, more data collection, and abstraction between the ruled and those ruling. The British reinvented how they could extract wealth from the colonies and that became a mechanized way of understanding government. The British Civil Service was the bureaucracy that ensured the mechanism of government ran smoothly. It was developed as a government machine to sustain colonialism. Early computing machines and the technocrats who advocated for more mechanization facilitated this work.

Agar explains that, as colonialism and state expansion further taxed the bureaucratic infrastructure of the British Civil Service, governmental reforms shifted to ensure that the civil servants were committed to generalizable work: exchangeable, well trained, but not specialized. The virtue of this work, in the eyes of the technocrats, was that anyone could be replaced. The government was supposed to run like a machine. The government machine of the British Civil Service became the social infrastructure that shaped and became the exigence for the invention of the computer. However, Agar is clear there was a division of labor: most civil servants worked diligently and precisely as (replaceable) generalists, but some civil servants were designated as experts, given a wide berth and creative latitude. In the twentieth century, these prestigious experts were technocrats who were given freedom and intellectual latitude to experiment.

All the men and women I introduce in this story were, in various ways, to this manner born. Turing, whose father held a high-ranking position in the British Civil Service in India, was born into this legacy of computation for state control. With the Second World War looming close, Turing quickly enlisted to aid in developing technologies that would further facilitate processing, interpreting, and controlling information networks. His inventions were put directly into the service of maintaining the expansive work of the British government, commerce, and control around the globe.

At the same time the British Empire was shrinking, so too was its ability to extract wealth from colonized people and land, hence so too was there a push to expand British dominance through computing. Historian of technology Mar Hicks explains,

> the computing revolution also offered Britain a final chance to reclaim the power of a fading empire and revive the flow of capital from overseas that it had enjoyed in the past. . . . Upgrading machines promised benefits of control rather than price, and supporting the British computing industry offered the possibility of once again raising Britain's global standing via technological innovation. (11–12)

The British government identified and expanded the controlling potential of computing technology. This historical context is of vital importance in order to trace and narrate the continued colonial logics encoded into digital computing and the entire social infrastructure out of which British computing industries emerged. In each subsequent chapter, I identify these colonial logics and the ways in which white colonial privileges enabled the work of these communities of women and of queer men.

However, I would not define my methodologies as decolonial. As Cana Uluak Itchuaqiyaq and Breeanne Matheson argue, the term *decolonial* is often applied as a metaphor stretched too thin to water down the impact of decolonial work ("Decolonizing Decoloniality"). By their definition, decolonial methodologies must center Indigenous concerns as well as directly benefit Indigenous communities. My research does not meet those expectations. I have learned, however, from scholars in Indigenous rhetorics and Indigenous technical communication scholarship, especially Qwo-Li Driskill's thinking on queer Indigenous gender and sexuality ("Decolonial Skillshares" and "Doubleweaving") as well as scholarship on technology by Angela Haas ("Race" and "Wampum") and on technical communication by Cana Uluak Itchuaqiyaq (Itchuaqiyaq and Matheson, "Decolonial" and Decolonizing"). From this work, I have shifted to consistently identify colonialism as central to the history of computing. I locate invention beyond the white dominant model to show the importance of community, culture, and materiality in the history of technologies broadly.

I focus on the embodied experiences of a few men and women, the richness of embodiment and affect. Embodiment is always composed within and through structural, political, and cultural contexts. It is my hope that by integrating structural context alongside individual embodiment, I articulate a nuanced portrait of the history of computing, one that includes both the power of hegemonic institutions as well as the particularity of unique people's experiences. To this end, embodiment is seen as shaped by hegemony and yet not entirely determined.

QUEERING TECHNICAL AND PROFESSIONAL WRITING
I submitted the complete manuscript of this book to the editors at NCTE during December 2022. One month later, the world of

writing studies and writing as a professional practice experienced one of the most challenging technological innovations in decades: ChatGPT. At first, some responded with punitive measures, designing new programs to identify AI-generated writing. Most teachers of writing I know responded by designing writing assignments that cannot easily be completed by AI. I am writing this less than a year from ChatGPT's introduction, and the current trends offer nuanced methods of teaching with and against ChatGPT, teaching a literacy for and alongside AI-based writing. I am sure that by the time the book is published, new best practices will have emerged, and new theories and ethics will be debated. By the time this book reaches your hands, the world of writing will be reshaped once again by technologies. The only certainty is that ChatGPT is changing and will continue to change the writing process for students, teachers, researchers, and writing professionals. Change is the constant. And I am not in the game of predicting the future.

I offer a historical grounding for AI writing that is, in a way, a queer origin story of AI writing. It is a history by way of a queer love story. I hope this book can offer an important historical background for a technology that some fear is going to dig up writing craft and teaching by its roots. In Chapter 3, I discuss and analyze the first computer-generated writing. This historical example of computer-generated writing reminds us that things could be otherwise: ChatGPT was not inevitable, and programmers in the past had very different values for the design of computer-generated writing. The assumed value of computing technology was, in the not-so-distant past, rather different from that of contemporary models. Use, efficacy, productivity—these were not the metrics of success. Instead, the queer men who worked on the early digital computers used them to play games and experiment. They taught the computer to sing songs and programmed it to write gender-neutral love letters that nearly scream with longing. The first computer-generated writing would make ChatGPT blush.

Beyond this current technological shift with AI writing, queer techné, as I analyze, invites us to think queerly and capriciously about the intersections of writing, bodies, and technologies. This embodied, intimate history of computing is an invitation to open new lines of research that further develop queer and embodied rhetorics within technical and scientific rhetorics. We have just begun to study the embodied and queer rhetorics within the rhetoric of science (Milbourne and Hallenbeck; Fountain; Teston) and in technical rhetorics (Jones et al; Fancher, "Composing"). Michael Faris called for the need for queer theory in technical communication in a series of provocative questions, including "To what degree is technical communication, implicitly and explicitly, invested in the reproduction of heteronormative culture and politics? . . . Alternatively, where is technical communication implicitly, in unstated and resistant ways, already queer?" ("Addressing"). Building on these questions, Jones et al. ended their antenarrative of technical communication by calling attention to all the work left to be done:

> We call for any work at all that acknowledges the need to queer technical communication and resist the binaries that continue to dominate the field. In short, we seek any and all TPC research and pedagogy that embraces perspectives and knowledges that do not necessarily assume an anticultural, Westernized, heteronormative, and patriarchal positionality. (223)

My research begins to answer that call by demonstrating how attuning ourselves to techné can result in a new, rich understanding of historical figures like Turing as well as the development of early digital computers. I offer queer techné as a frame for locating embodiment and queer desire within technological discourses. My hope is that scholars continue this work. I wonder what other communities and sites of technological innovation might have an undercurrent of queer desire, queer longing? What other queer communities are celebrated for invention and did so through playful, useless, or erotic energy? Can we approach technical writing with longing? I wonder how queer desire might be both explored and stymied by programs like ChatGPT. Queer desire for

ChatGPT can direct these questions: What desire can be written, in what terms, and toward what ends? How many thousands of our beloved copyrighted queer texts have trained AI-generative writing programs? And what did the program learn from digesting the great works of queer literature? How could ChatGPT possibly integrate Jeanette Winterson? I want to imagine that the power of Ocean Vuong or Carmen Maria Machado could break the algorithm, but I doubt that hope is realistic.

Jones and colleagues identify queer technical communication as that which resists binaries. Queer techné resists stable knowledge itself and reminds us of the unknowability and unpredictability of both math and computing. Resistance is not the only component of queer technical communication. When we resist heteronormativity, we also open new ways of being with one another, new pleasures, and greater experiences for joy.

I wrote this book because we need queer stories. I mean this in two ways. First, we need stories of queer people. The queer stories that I want need not be hero stories; these people are flawed, complicit in systems of oppression, and all of them made technical breakthroughs that were on the horizon in other places as well. But these people are interesting because they bring their bodies into their technical work. The women brought their embodied knowledge as experts in operating computers. They also leveraged their lifetime of practice with feminine comportment to navigate the male-dominated social and technical space. Turing is interesting for the sheer creativity and strangeness of his technical thinking. And the queer community, as a group of trusted friends, is fascinating for the way they weave sexuality and research, erotics and intelligence, through their letters.

Second, we need stories that are themselves queer. These stories refuse to be easily defined, resist easy telling, and leave us perhaps a bit unsettled. I want queer stories that make us question our desires, technologies, writing processes, and friendships. Queer stories, it is my hope, will never become gospel truth, but they will linger with my readers. Perhaps queer techné will leave us desiring more questions.

I need queer stories. I grew up as a Jehovah's Witness, a religion that taught me that all homosexuality is not just a sin but also a perversion. When I was caught being intimate with my girlfriends, we were shamed. We were told we were dirty. With weekly instruction by a group of Elders, I learned to accept the shame they heaped on my body. I had to travel far from home before I was able to imagine queer affection in the daylight.

I was on a bus from the airport to my hostel in Madrid for a summer of study abroad through college. This was my first trip out of the country and my first time spending more than a couple of days without the insular community of Jehovah's Witnesses. My feet had not even touched Spanish soil when I saw something that cracked the religious worldview, letting light flood in to illuminate my latent questions.

As our bus stopped at a red light, I saw two men holding hands on the street corner below me. They brushed a light kiss and parted ways. In my imagination, they headed to their respective offices, likely to meet again in the evening at that same corner to walk home. Never in my life had I seen gay affection like this: public and unashamed.

What I saw on that street corner in Madrid was nothing like my experience of pleasure and love. These Spanish men were public, casual, and poignant exactly because their display of affection was also mundane. At 9 a.m., no one on the street seemed to see, notice, or think anything was special about this kiss. The light turned green, the bus pulled away, and men continued with their days. I was left to wonder whether life might not at all be what I had assumed it could be. I wanted to know their story. I wanted to know their love story and watch the peace of their day-to-day life as openly queer men. I began to imagine that my own story could look a little like theirs. My story could still be otherwise to what I had been taught.

We need an embodied, queer counterhistory of computing to remind us that things can be otherwise. These communities existed within and were upheld by dominant, masculinist, and colonial systems. That much is known and certain. At the same time, their embodied knowledge was not completely determined by those systems. Embodied knowledge of queer techné offers something different. There is a space in which to be otherwise and even abundant at times.

My own queer techné embodiment animates my research. Queer techné has become a process of living in and then out of the closet, searching for queer community and learning to trust that the desires I have can teach me about my body, mind, and world. Throughout this book, I integrate my own queer stories so that I situate my research in relationship to my own life. While I had to go searching for Turing's queer techné, I have made my own queer techné explicit and visible in each chapter of this book. Integrating my own queer techné into this research was a challenge at first. I often publish creative personal essays for magazines and literary journals. These personal accounts are read by hundreds of thousands of people. And I share them with ease. And yet I struggled to bring my personal narrative into this research. I have been so well-trained by academic publishing to separate the subject of research from the author researching. But the subject of this research—techné—is close to my skin and enlivened by my lived experience. Previous generations of queer scholars have taught me how to integrate the personal into the scholarship, especially the personal narratives of Jacqueline Rhodes and Jonathan Alexander in *Techne*, as well as autoethnography as queer methodology, as, for instance, in Michael Faris's "Queering Networked Writing" and J. Logan Smilges's *Queer Silence: On Disability and Rhetorical Absence*. A long history of queer scholars in rhetoric has taught me that we need not erase our personal narratives, in all of their embodied richness, from our research.

I want you, my reader, to leave this story thinking about the history of computers not as a technical, dry narrative; rather, it was full of feeling, love, care, frustration, and negotiation. Through this research project, I invite you to think about invention and technical writing as shot through with desire and hope.

CHAPTER OVERVIEW

In the following chapter, I analyze the technical and scientific writing of Alan Turing, who lived as a relatively open gay man in a time when antigay laws were enforced with imprisonment or chemical therapy. He lived his life navigating in and out of the closet, and his life depended on it. His experience in this repressive culture shaped his queer identity, and because of this, Turing's technical writing includes queer techné. This chapter includes close analysis of Turing's two most influential articles, "On Computable Numbers" and "Computing Machinery and Intelligence," and integrates narratives from Turing's life. These close analyses and biographical narratives coalesce to demonstrate the ways that Turing's embodied techné shaped and enriched his theoretical writing and his contributions to early digital computing. In addition, Chapter 2 outlines key places in his technical writing where queer rhetoric constitutes his inventive, forward-thinking theories on digital computation and artificial intelligence. This chapter offers a significant contribution to technical communication and technical rhetoric by locating epistemologies of the closet and queer rhetorics in technical communication.

In Chapter 3, I use archival research to identify a queer network of friends who collaborated on early computer programming and computer science. This group of queer friends set the machine to work on an entirely unusual set of tasks: singing, reading, and writing poetry. This may seem like a strange choice, but when we look more closely at the community of people working on this computer and their competing interests, we can begin to understand. In particular, the technical writing makes visible the queer techné of this community, including collaboration, play, experimentation, and desire that animate early experiments in computer programming.

In the fourth chapter, I return to writing about women and computers. Women were the primary operators and often the primary programmers for early computers in England during and after World War II, well into the 1960s. The logbooks, operation manuals, and instruction sets all record the contributions of women. I argue that the primary social infrastructure of early digital computing was built on the embodied techné of women. This labor has been erased due in part to sexism and, in related part, to the fact that the technical writing of these women has been dismissed as "merely technical" and not as serious intellectual work (Jack, *Science*). This chapter theorizes embodied techné as both embodiment and technical expertise. Through the everyday, physical processes of operating, struggling, fixing, and negotiating with the computer, these women cultivated embodied knowledge that was vital to the development and improvement of the computer. As scholars of technical writing strive to be more inclusive, this chapter demonstrates that an attention to embodied techné can recover the intellectual and technical contributions of often invisible labor, especially those of women.

I conclude by recognizing that while queer techné has shaped invention in the history of computing, queer techné has also shaped my own research process. In the final chapter, I reflect on the significance of each preceding chapter. I locate how my own embodied experience and queer techné have shaped my archival methods, my arguments, and my commitments as a writer. Thus, I theorize the significance of queer techné as archival methodology. Through this final chapter, I hope readers are inspired to locate the queer techne that enlivens their own research, their writing, and the archives of our lives.

2

Embodying Turing's Machine

ALAN TURING IS WIDELY RECOGNIZED, celebrated, and debated[2] as a "founding father" of digital computation. His early contribution to digital computing was a theoretical innovation he published in the 1936 article "On Computable Numbers, with an Application to the Entscheidungsproblem." This article has been called a foundational text for innovating digital computation and for conceptually separating the hardware of a computing machine from the software of its programming (Copeland, *Essential Turing* 5–10; Isaacson 43–46). We have almost no records of how Turing developed his innovative ideas. There are no drafts, no notes, nor any early presentations. Although mathematicians had been puzzling over this same math theorem for decades, Turing appears to have developed his solution quickly over just a few short weeks during his summer break between graduating with his master's degree and beginning his first teaching position.

Many years later, when Turing was an established mathematician, an admiring graduate student asked Turing how he developed his ideas in "On Computable Numbers." Turing answered with a story: he went for a run on a warm summer day, lay in a field, and gazed at the clouds. And it hit him. He had figured it out!

So goes the story. (See Figure 3.)

In this chapter, I pull Turing's ideas from the clouds and place them more firmly on the ground. As a runner myself, I am curious about Turing's running and physical training as an essential component of his invention process. Turing's narrative, though charming, conceals more than it reveals. The lone, male genius struck with a eureka moment has long been a myth of knowledge

Figure 3: Photograph of Alan Turing running; inscribed on back: "National Physical Lab. 2nd in 3 miles." Photo dated December 26, 1946.

production. And this myth reifies a model of epistemology in which knowledge is universal, stable, and context-free. Turing's story also reifies a notion of knowledge production that separates bodies and minds, asserting that invention occurs in the mind alone and is separated from the embodied practices of techné that shape intellectual work.

Turing's theories and inventions helped move computation out of the hands of men and women and into computers. He argued that machines, not just humans of flesh and blood, could perform intelligence. For these accomplishments, he has long been identified as a key figure in widening the chasm between bodies and minds. In different ways, this has been argued by Jay David Bolter, Katherine N. Hayles, Friedrich Kittler, and Wendy Chun. Turing's own invention story supports these critics and the role they cast for him in the narrative separating bodies and minds.

However, a closer look at Turing's technical writing shows a more fully embodied story. We see his queer process, with a uniquely queer techné appearing as central to his intellectual work. Using a similar method as Jennifer Lin LeMesurier's study of somatic metaphors, I identify traces of embodiment and embodied experience in Alan Turing's writing. Embodiment, according to LeMesurier, is rhetorically potent even when physical bodies are not seen or felt taking up physical space. She defines a "body"

> as a functional, inventional actor and bearer of ideological weight, capable of producing rhetorical influence. This parsing of the moving, sensing, biological body is not an attempt to reaffirm idealist/materialist binaries. Rather, my goal is to perceive how symbolic systems and bodies are always already intertwined so as to better understand what embodied and material effects are already present but unaccounted for in rhetorical work. (363)

LeMesurier performs her method of identifying the somatic metaphors that form traces of the rhetorical influence of embodied experience, feeling, movement, and training. This aspect of defining embodied rhetoric is significant because it means that all texts are, to varying degrees, shaped by embodied rhetoric—all texts are composed by and for bodies.

I argue that Turing's writing and his theoretical and technical innovations are examples of embodied rhetoric: his embodied experiences are the ground upon which his theoretically and technically inventive thinking was built. Furthermore, I identify Turing's embodied rhetoric as a queer techné because Turing's writing practices resist the dominant assumptions about mathematics, as well as machine intelligence, that were most widely held at the time and continue to hold sway. In this chapter, I isolate the analysis of Alan Turing and his writing. I focus on him as a solo writer and inventor to show the deep connections between embodiment, sexuality, and scientific invention. While this chapter is exclusively about Turing, he was no isolated genius. His knowledge was composed within communities, and the next chapter locates that community in detail. This chapter focuses on one person's embodied experience. In the following chapters, I connect the personal to the community.

Judith Butler's influential early essay "Performative Acts and Gender Constitution: An Essay in Phenomenology and Feminist Theory" theorizes phenomenology of gender in order to first introduce the concept of performativity. Butler is often misunderstood, oversimplified. Performativity has been conflated with performance: an act, a show, putting on gender and its style. Rather, in Butler's theories, performativity is the act of becoming by doing. We become gendered by doing gender. Likewise, bodies are unbecoming by undoing genders. Bodies are at the same time sites of oppression and sites of creativity and invention. I find this early text important to return to in my analysis because Butler considers the inventive potential for gender performativity: "As a corporeal field of cultural play, gender is a basically innovative affair, although it is quite clear that there are strict punishments for contesting the script by performing out of turn or through unwarranted improvisations" ("Performative Acts" 361). Gender is re-seen as an *innovative affair*. Like techné, gender becomes by doing, and out of that doing, we can both reify norms as well as resist them. Performativity offers the possibility to innovate and invent.

In *Bodies That Matter*, Butler further defines and analyzes performativity as a central site of struggle. That tension is played out on our bodies—both bodies disciplined by gendered politics and bodies as inventive, creative even, of new gendering experiences. Butler reminds us that "bodies never quite comply" (2). The disciplined performances of our bodily styles are never perfectly applied, performed, or regulated. Gender can be a techné, a practice that both reproduces and invents.

In a similar vein, Turing was surely disciplined into the conventions of mathematics, which enforce disembodied, objective standards for writing. He was also disciplined into a culture of heteronormativity and homophobia. Yet his close friend Norman Routledge said of his intellectual and personal characteristics that "it's the fact that he was so original. He's so untouched by fashion and was totally his own man. This is why he was able to make the breakthrough that he did" ("Norman Routledge - Being Friends"). Turing's tendency to be "untouched by fashion" extended into his writing, which is often creative, affective, and less formal than most mathematical theory. I find that Turing's embodied experience and his rhetorical strategies do not comply with disciplinary conventions for producing and composing knowledge.

Turing became famous for his inventive work on computing, and even in this work he was creative and surprising. In these universal computing machines, an inventor would hope for a high degree of regularity and conformity. But, while he argued that machines could think, Turing recalled how "machines surprise me with great frequency" ("Computing Machinery" 455). And these surprises were, for him, a positive thing. The surprises were signs that maybe machines could eventually think. Turing asks us to have a similarly generous awareness of the subtle differences, outliers, and surprises that our technologies perform. Bodies, writing, and machines: we do not comply . . . not totally. His texts are lively with embodied experience, and his arguments leave questions open and prevent conclusive answers. Turing's embodied, queer rhetoric reminds us to look for surprises and to enjoy those surprises.

I identify Turing's queer, embodied techné by analyzing two of his most famous articles: "On Computable Numbers, with an

Application to the Entscheidungsproblem," published in 1936, and "Computing Machinery and Intelligence" from 1950. I also relate these texts to Turing's life by drawing on Andrew Hodges's extensive biography, *Alan Turing: The Enigma*. In my analysis, I locate embodied rhetoric from Turing's first influential article on theoretical mathematics, in which he theorizes the possibility of a digital computer well before its invention. Then I build on this to identify queer techné in his most famous essay on artificial intelligence, published in 1950, shortly after the first digital computers were in operation. Together, these articles allow me to identify the important role of Turing's embodied experiences for developing his innovative thinking on digital computing.

THE TURING MACHINE: QUEER TECHNÉ AND EPISTEMOLOGY

In 1935, Alan Turing was a recent graduate of King's College Cambridge and unsure of where his life would take him next. He completed his bachelor's degree in advanced mathematics and was given a fellowship at Cambridge, which gave him a small salary and the extensive time to continue his research (Hodges 94–95). During the summer after graduation, Turing made good use of this time by drafting the article "On Computable Numbers, with an Application to the Entscheidungsproblem," which addresses an abstract problem in logical mathematics. I argue that embodied experiences, and queer techné in particular, are the starting place for solving abstract theoretical problems and innovating theoretical foundations for digital computation.

In "On Computable Numbers," Alan Turing first demonstrates that mathematics is not a decidable science, which means that there may always be problems that cannot be solved. To make this conclusion, Turing also theorizes the Turing machine, which was later attributed as a theoretical foundation for digital computation. Until 1936, David Hilbert and most prominent mathematicians theorized that every mathematical question could be solved given precise terms. Turing demonstrates that mathematics is not, in fact, capable of deciding or resolving every mathematical problem through effective method.

To understand the significance of both Turing's arguments and his method of developing his arguments, it is vital to understand the context of mathematics at the time. For the first half of the twentieth century, David Hilbert represented the old guard of modernist logic and mathematics. In 1901, Hilbert set the agenda for mathematics by defining what he considered to be the pressing problems the field needed to solve. The three most significant problems were the following: "Is mathematics complete?," "Is mathematics consistent?," and "Is mathematics decidable?" Hilbert posited these as questions, but he also assumed that the answers were all yes. His challenge was to positively affirm these assumptions. The program for mathematics, as Hilbert defined it, was to prove that mathematics is complete, consistent, and decidable (Copeland, *Essential Turing* 46–47; Hodges 91; Leavitt 40). Hilbert hoped these universal principles of mathematics would create order and control out of an otherwise chaotic world (Leavitt 40–41). They were entering a new century, and it would be a century of order, logic, and reason. Mathematics was seen as the key to ensuring a more logical future world order.

For Hilbert, the mathematical and logical universal forms were there to be discovered. He was, as Turing biographer David Leavitt points out, a Neo-Platonist (39). Logic and mathematical axioms were Absolute True forms that existed above and beyond any human experience. These axioms needed to be discovered through rigorous methods of logical proof. Hilbert metaphorically referred to mathematics as a paradise of logic and reason. He and his school of mathematicians wanted, above all else, logic, reason, and formalism to create order out of chaos and to let peace win out over the devastating losses of war. But the twentieth century brought many challenges to the hoped-for complete mathematics. And two world wars ended the dream of securing greater order and reason.

After World War I, a younger cohort of mathematicians began to trouble the waters in mathematics. In 1931, while Turing was a first-year student at King's College, Kurt Gödel falsified Hilbert's first two problems, finding that mathematics is not complete and not consistent (*On Formally Undecidable Propositions*). Gödel instigated a paradigm shift within mathematics: mathematics would never solve all problems without drawing from nonmathematical means of signification, formalism, and information. With these theorems, Gödel showed that the paradise of mathematical truth would always have snakes that lurk in trees.

The older group of mathematicians held the idealist notion that reason would bring order and peace, if rational humans could only apply mathematical principles appropriately (Leavitt 39). That was the dream in 1900. By 1936, with one world war past and another on the horizon, the hope that universal forms could bring order and peace to human knowledge and human civilization was gone. The younger generation of men would go on to play some part in World War II, working on everything from cryptology to computers to atom bombs. This generation of mathematicians took disorder, chaos, and paradox as an unavoidable given.

Gödel's theories falsified Hilbert's first two questions. But mathematics continued to have the authority of decidability, the *Entscheidungsproblem*. In other words, when given enough time and the correct procedure, mathematics could always find a solution to mathematical problems. Gödel felt there must be a way to falsify this claim, and he worked (unsuccessfully) for more than a decade to find the logical proof. In 1935, just after graduating from King's College Cambridge, young Turing turned his attention to the Entscheidungsproblem. Almost inadvertently, his proof for falsifying this theorem generated the concept of the Turing machine.

Turing's "On Computable Numbers" accomplishes two primary things. First and most intentionally, he proves that the problem of decidability can never be solved by *effective method*, which is the method of logical and mathematical proof in which problems are solved. Second, to make this conclusion, Turing proposes a universal computing machine, which became a significant theoretical foundation for the digital computer.

Turing scholar Jack Copeland stresses that Turing's argument specifically addresses mathematics through effective method ("Narrow" 12–13). Copeland finds that scholars most often get this point wrong in that they conflate effective method of calculation with *all* methods of calculation. Copeland clarifies that some mathematical problems are not solvable through effective method. The key difference is that Turing proved that effective methods (or computable methods) cannot solve some mathematical problems. As Hodges explains, the question is, "did there exist a definite method which could, in principle, be applied to any assertion, and which was guaranteed to produce a correct decision as to whether that assertion was true?" (91). To solve this problem, Turing turned toward embodiment in the process of computing, a radical shift both methodologically and theoretically.

Closer analysis of Turing's text reveals that his embodied experiences are central to his thinking process and rhetorical strategies. As Jennifer Lin LeMesurier argues, "The moving body as both responder and creator can be considered a material rhetorical device that (a) influences other bodies' uptake of bodily knowledge and (b) uses its own knowledge and forces, ever shifting in the albumen of bodily encounters, to yield rhetorical effects" (378). The traces of Turing's bodily experience, as both responder and creator, can be found in the rhetorical effects of his article. His body's experiences include everyday experience, such as calculating problems and navigating bodily needs for food and rest. These embodied experiences shape Turing's rhetorical strategies as well as his theories.

Embodied rhetoric appears in "On Computable Numbers" when Turing first introduces the computing machine, which, at first, is a human computer. He introduces what became known as the Turing machine: "We may compare a man in the process of computing a real number to a machine" (59). As he develops this argument, he begins with the embodied practice of computing: "Computing is normally done by writing certain symbols on paper. We may suppose this paper is divided into squares like a child's arithmetic book" (75). Although he does not specify any particular person, this computing man would have been familiar to Turing in two different ways: (1) the typical model of a computer would have been a woman's white-collar work, and (2) Turing himself would have spent many hours performing calculations.

As a young mathematician working on an independent, theoretical problem, Turing performed computing tasks for himself. Day in and day out, he spent his time writing calculations on physical paper. The process would be familiar to him and to his audience. This familiar human process becomes the model upon which he would propose the Turing machine.

Turing develops "On Computable Numbers" in a way that attends to computing as embodied work. Specifically, he begins accounting for the unique bodily limitations and needs of human computers: "It is always possible for the computer to break off from his work, to go away and forget all about it, and later to come back and go on with it. If he does this, he must leave a note of instructions, written in some standard form" (79). This computing man is given a complex calculation, which would be typical and tedious. These calculations would take any man a long time, which means he would have to take breaks. Turing notes that, before breaking, the computer would need to write down instructions for himself or herself "in some standard form" in order to know what to do next. Then Turing suggests that this computer is especially lazy: "Suppose that the computer works in such a desultory manner that he never does more than one step at a sitting" (79). This computer must get up after each step, perhaps to get a drink of water or to stretch. Therefore, each step of the calculation must be written down in the most basic terms.

Obviously, as Turing's reasoning continues, this lazy man writing down instructions would not be efficient at solving any mathematical proof. To replace this hypothetical, desultory worker, Turing describes a kind of machine that can read an infinitely long tape of paper, write 0 or 1, and move that tape from right to left. With these simple functions, Turing describes his Turing machine. He uses the bodily needs to stand up, take breaks, and even engage in lazy work habits as an important rhetorical step to first separate hardware—the human computer—from software—the standard form instructions of noting each step of the calculation. These instructions for each step become the prototype for computer programming.

Turing's peers found his "On Computable Numbers, with an Application to the Entscheidungsproblem" and, in particular, his method of embodying the process of computation to be highly unusual. Hodges notes: "[I]t was not only a matter of abstract mathematics, not only a play of symbols, for it involved thinking about what people did in the physical world" (107). When Turing's professor of mathematics Max Newman read Turing's draft, Newman "could hardly believe that so simple and direct an idea as the Turing machine would answer the Hilbert problem over which many had been laboring for five years since Gödel had disposed of the other Hilbert questions" (Hodges 112). Its originality can be seen most clearly when comparing it to Alfonzo Church's method for solving the problem of decidability, which was published just a few short months before Turing's article. Church and Turing arrived at the same conclusion. However, Church's reasoning remains in the realm of abstract mathematical proofs with no connection or application to the material world (Copeland, *Essential Turing* 44–45).

By starting with the embodied experience of calculation, Turing ties mathematical theory directly to the concrete, embodied process of computing. Hodges describes this article as "the necessary bridge between the world of logic and the world in which people did things" (125). Turing first makes this connection between the embodied experience of computing and then builds on that to suggest a hypothetical computing machine. In doing so, he both solves a long-standing problem of theoretical mathematics (which Church's method also did) and outlines the theoretical foundations that would help to later separate code from physical computing.

Additionally, I find that Turing's logic in this essay reflects queer ways of knowing. Eve Sedgwick argues for the significance of accounting for sexuality in the work of knowledge production when she opens *Epistemology of the Closet*, asserting "an understanding of virtually any aspect of modern Western culture must be, not merely incomplete, but damaged in its central substance to the degree that it does not incorporate a critical analysis of modern homo/heterosexual definition" (1). This is not to say that Turing's inventions and theories are reducible to products of a queer sexuality (although Lassègue attempts to posit this in "What Kind of Turing Test Did Turing Have in Mind?"). Rather, accounting for knowledge production is always intertwined with a complex network of practices, institutions, and interpersonal dynamics that include the practices, institutions, and power relations disciplining homosexual and heterosexual subjects.

This epistemology of the closet is a productive, inventive way of knowing, even if that inventiveness is born out of a survival strategy. As Sedgwick argues in "Paranoid Reading and Reparative Reading," queer lives can and should be read for their reparative and even restorative, affirmative potential (147–50). Sedgwick finds that the "hermeneutics of suspicion" are the modus operandi of critical and cultural theory. Starting with suspicion has

> had an unintentionally stultifying side effect: [it] may have made it less rather than more possible to unpack the local, contingent relations between any given piece of knowledge and its narrative/epistemological entailments for the seeker, knower, or teller (124).

I note this same trend within theories of technoculture that are exclusively critical of Turing, as if his work can exclusively contribute to the separation between mind and body. From a hermeneutics of suspicion, it is too easy to overlook the "local, contingent relations" out of which Turing composed new knowledge and inventions that have become foundational in computer science and the history of digital computation. These local contingent relations include the details of his texts, the physical and cultural context in which he wrote, his unique embodied experience, and the broader intersubjective networks that are narratively and epistemically potent. From a reparative impulse, which "wants to assemble and confer plentitude" (Sedgewick, "Paranoid Reading" 149), we can find an abundance of queer affection, play, and invention within Turing's early writing.

When I read his text with an eye toward queer plentitude, I see that Turing arrives at his conclusion by focusing on the exception to the rule. On the one hand, he theorizes a definite method for mechanizing computation. He also identifies contradictions—especially the Halting Problem[3]—that remind us that mechanized computation through definite method is inherently limited and imperfect. Turing offers the Halting Problem as one problem that cannot be solved through effective methods. If a computer (either human or machine) were given the Halting Problem, the computer could calculate the problem but would never reach a conclusion. If a single person were calculating the problem, the time spent calculating and the accuracy of the calculation would necessarily be limited. On the other hand, when Turing replaces each activity of a human computer with a machine, the machine can run infinitely. In the case of the Halting Problem, the computer would run infinitely because the problem would circulate back repetitively, never reaching a conclusion. Turing started with embodied experience. These embodied experiences led him to see that there would always be questions without any answers.

McKinley Green identifies queer technical communication by locating unruly strategies that are forms of queer resistance. First, he defines resistance as a central queer rhetorical practice, especially resistance to user designs. Queering can include "elisions and gaps when emerging technologies and embodied experiences fail to align, instances when individuals intentionally refuse technology-based initiatives or subvert systems designed to include them" ("Resistance" 331–32). Building on this, he identifies queer rhetorics as definitionally unruly, in which users create practices and ways of relating that negotiate risk, intimacy, and community care outside of standard practices. These users are not acting in ignorance of best practices. Rather, knowing the standard best practices, they choose to enact their own sets of practices outside of set boundaries. Green specifically identifies unruly practices in queer youth HIV disclosure practices on Grindr. From his analysis, Green argues, "Unruliness acknowledges that individuals do not merely acquiesce to the risk-reduction messaging shaping digital designs like Grindr but subvert and redeploy those digital tools in ways that reflect contextual understandings of health, HIV, and risk" ("Risking Disclosure" 275). In this case, unruliness includes practices of resistance, subversion, and redeployment. So, while queering practices in technical communication previously have been defined by their antinormative, resistant, and unruly characteristics, by redeploying, queer practices are made generative and playful.

Turing's conclusion is the end to the imagined dream of mathematics as a garden of logic, order, and control posited by Hilbert and an entire school of mathematics. Therefore, scholar of queer history and technology Jacob Gaboury locates Turing's work as a queer foundation in the history of digital computation ("On Uncomputable Numbers"). Gaboury defines *queerness* as a method not an object, and that method opposes productivity, stability, and legibility. From this point of view, Turing's theoretical work queers: his ideas resist totalizing, complete answers. In both style and theoretical significance, Turing's queer, embodied rhetorics can be seen as resistant or noncompliant with the dominant, disciplinary conventions of mathematics. Turing's conclusion resisted the notion that mathematical progress was inherently stable, pure, and knowable, and it contributed to a paradigm shift in mathematics (Hodges 84–86).

Mathematics will always have problems. Solving them will always require creativity, and Turing looked forward to that surprising, creative work. The embodied experience of calculating problems allowed him to argue that mathematics is not nearly so stable and universal as Hilbert hypothesized. By starting with that embodied techné, Turing was able to clear the theoretical air. In the end, embodied and queer techné were productive sources of knowledge that framed Turing's thinking as he resisted the disciplinary conventions of the time and affirmed the importance of practical, embodied experience for technological innovation.

THE TURING TEST: QUEERING INTELLIGENCE

Turing's mentor, Max Newman, became the head of the Computing Machine Laboratory at the University of Manchester and began work on building an early computer in 1946. By 1948 the

Manchester Mark I, nicknamed "the Baby," was fully operational. In the same year, Newman recruited Turing to collaborate in the computing lab. Later, Norbert Wiener traveled from the United States to see the Mark I (see Figure 4) and to talk to Turing. From this exchange, Wiener was emboldened in his belief that machines could be developed to replicate or even replace human bodies, an idea he published in his widely circulated book from 1950, *The Human Use of Human Beings*. Turing held a more modest belief. He did not imagine that machines would replace humans. However, in his 1950 essay, "Computing Machinery and Intelligence," he did imagine that machines could think. Therefore, he explored nontraditional definitions of intelligence and challenged traditional notions of humanity.

By 1950, Turing was in a different place in his life. He was no longer the young, promising mathematician and now had an established career. After successfully publishing "On Computable Numbers," he completed his PhD at Princeton University in 1938 under the mentorship of Alfonzo Church. During World War II, Turing established his professional and intellectual legacy through his work as a code breaker and mathematician, and he developed early versions of computers for British intelligence warfare. In 1948, Turing became the deputy director of the Computing Laboratory at the University of Manchester. He had the freedom there to experiment with the potential of digital computation. Before too long, Turing's computers were programmed to sing songs and write poems.

Whether or not "the Baby" was ready, the press picked up on the developments under way in the University of Manchester Computing Lab. Turing became an important advocate of this machine's development. In addition to complex mathematical calculations, he and his colleagues taught the Manchester computers human languages, songs, and poetry. During a radio broadcast, a reporter brought children to see and hear "the Baby" try to sing popular songs. The technicians explained that the computer was also learning to play chess. A reporter who interviewed Turing cited Turing's goals as "the investigation of the possibilities of machines

Figure 4: Photograph of Manchester Mark I with labeled components published in *The Illustrated London News*, June 25, 1949.

for their own sake . . . and to what extent it could think for itself" (Hodges 406). Although this was more moderate than Wiener's goal of replacing human bodies, the general public did not receive news of Turing's work and the computer at Manchester with open arms (Hodges 404). Sir Geoffrey Jefferson, a prominent neurologist at the University of Manchester, published a widely read critique of Turing's work. He argues that Turing's intelligent machine is a threat to the humanist-exclusive claim on intelligence. Jefferson's arguments reveal that Turing's machine and his writing were received with anxiety and to some were perceived as threatening.

In 1948, Jefferson published the article "Mind of the Mechanical Man" in the *British Medical Journal,* which circulated widely. Jefferson begins by addressing the question of the relation between brain and mind. He was a renowned expert on this topic, innovating neurosurgery during and following World War II. Jefferson saw firsthand how physical, neurological, and psychological trauma affected not just the brain but also the mind and body in different ways. In his discussion of mind and brain, Jefferson argues that human intelligence is directly connected to embodied experience. He then goes on to argue for a version of true intelligence that would be unattainable by machines—creative, emotional, and even sensory (the machine could at best hope to be a parrot spitting back a few lines it could learn).

Jefferson concludes that, even if we could build an intelligent machine, to do so would be inherently antihumanist, an affront to the centrality and superiority of humanity. He defends a strong humanist notion in which intelligence is the sole property of humans and excludes any machine and all animals. This is so, for Jefferson, because the human brain is completely and unexplainably unique: "its functions may be mimicked by machines, [but the human mind] remains itself and is unique in Nature" (1106). For Jefferson, humanity is the definition of intelligence, and intelligence is the defining quality of humanity.

What qualifies humans to be the sole possessor of thought and intelligence? Jefferson defines intelligence as the whole range of human experience of pleasure, pain, and even love and sex. In particular, he identifies language use and the ability to use language to advance human knowledge as the thing that sets humans apart from even the highest animals. According to Jefferson,

> Not until a machine can write a sonnet or compose a concerto because of thoughts and emotions felt, and not by the chance fall of symbols, could we agree that machine equals brain—that is, not only write it, but know that it had written it. No mechanism could feel (and not merely artificially signal, an easy contrivance) pleasure at its successes, grief when its valves fuse, be warmed by flattery, be made miserable by its mistakes, be charmed by sex, be angry or depressed when it cannot get what it wants. (1110)

A machine may be able to spit out correct answers or repeat stock phrases, but intelligence requires a full range of embodied and discursive behaviors. A machine could never have these things; therefore, a machine cannot be said to think.

At the heart of Jefferson's argument we find a humanist argument and the human body. The embodied experiences of humans—our experiences, passions, and emotions—constitute intelligence. However, Jefferson's primary critique is that the human mind has something, some soul-like essence, that is always more than bodies and always unexplainable through material sciences.

Turing responded in 1950 in the article "Computing Machinery and Intelligence" published in *Mind*. In this essay, which reads like a manifesto, Turing agrees with many of Jefferson's points. He agrees that the analogy between human brains and computing machinery is weak insofar as human brains and bodies are far more complex. In addition, Turing agrees that human intelligence is a product, in part, of our embodied experiences and emotions. However, Turing then shifts the conversation.

Compared to his earlier theoretical article "On Computable Numbers," Turing's writing style in "Computing Machinery and Intelligence," his most widely read publication then and now, is both surprisingly clear and entertaining for an article by a mathematician. For example, when addressing objections, Turing writes with grace and wit: "We do not wish to penalize the machine for its inability to shine in beauty competitions, nor to penalize a man for losing in a race against an aeroplane. The conditions of our game make these disabilities irrelevant" (442). Turing goes on to address, point by point, common objections that were raised most directly by Geoffrey Jefferson. Turing weaves philosophical, rhetorical, and technical questions that invite consideration of the potential for machine intelligence.

To defend the possibility of machine intelligence, Turing defines intelligence through a broader set of embodied experiences. What is especially significant is that when Turing moves to defend machine intelligence, he not only humanizes computing machinery, but he also genders computers as feminine. And this gendered aspect is far from a tangent: gendered and sexualized performances are integral to Turing's thinking and his knowledge production.

The first way that Turing embodies this intelligent machine is with a test of gender identity. Turing opens by replacing the question "Can machines think?" with a more specific question tested through an imitation game. To introduce this imitation game, Turing starts with a gendered one: "It is played with three people, a man (A), a woman (B), and an interrogator (C) who may be of either sex. The interrogator stays in a room apart from the other two. The object of the game for the interrogator is to determine which of the two is the man and which is the woman" ("Computing Machinery" 441). The interrogator can ask the man and woman questions, but the interrogator can neither see nor hear the participants. In this game, deception is the rule. Apparently, the trick is that the woman is supposed to be honest, and the man seeks to trick the interrogator: "it is A's object in the game to try and cause C to make the wrong identification" (441). After establishing this first game of gendered deception, Turing switches the man for a computer: "What will happen when a machine takes the part of A in the game? Will the interrogator decide wrongly as often when the game is played like this as he does when the game is played between a man and a woman? These questions replace our original, 'Can machines think?'" (441). Read literally, machine intelligence is parallel to a man pretending to be a woman. Here, in one of the earliest and most well-read essays on the future of machine intelligence, we have gender performance, a man pretending to be a woman and a machine also pretending to be a woman. We have artificial intelligence as gender fluidity.

This passage is the most obviously queer expression of artificial intelligence in Turing's essay. Turing assumes that gender is performative and compares the performance of gender to the performance of intelligence. However, in contemporary versions of this test, gender is frequently erased (Copeland and Proudfoot; Schnelle; Whitby). Turing biographer Andrew Hodges quickly assumes Turing's use of gender as unnecessary to the general concept, in that it is a distracting choice, a red herring (415). There has been a long tradition of erasing the gendered component of Turing's test. Even Turing, in "Can Automatic Calculating Machines Be Said to Think?," erases the gendered aspect of the test in later arguments for mechanical intelligence.

Turing's gender game is of crucial importance for understanding both him and artificial intelligence. Alan Clinton explicitly makes this claim:

> Although the purpose of the paper was to explore the possibilities of artificial intelligence, a side effect of Turing's formulation is the implication that "man" and "woman" are already simulations, an accumulation of codes. Who is more apt at producing the "correct" or "convincing" answers may vary more according to the rhetorical skills of the participants than to their biology (or lack thereof). From this moment on, digital technology's association with gender-bending, its aptitude for queerness, was ineradicably grounded. (218)

Clinton identifies Turing's gendered game as a founding moment for queering in digital computing. Turing's game introduces gender-bending into digital computing. But this opening analogy is not the only queering that Turing encodes into his argument.

Additionally, throughout Turing's article, I find that Turing queers computing by integrating queer techné, actions of gender-bending and gender ambiguity. He weaves gendering performances into his entire defense of machine intelligence and by extension genders intelligence as well. In particular, the computing intelligence continues to enact femininity and practices associated with femininity.

He includes feminizing phrases and metaphors throughout this article. He asks, "[W]ill X please tell me the length of his or her hair?" ("Computing Machinery" 441) and writes, "we do not wish to penalize the machine for its inability to shine in beauty competitions" (442). Here, Turing humorously imagines how poorly his computer will perform when evaluated for its physical beauty. Both questions for intelligence are feminized.

When considering what qualifies as intelligence, Turing writes a lovely list of behaviors that qualify as intelligence but that the machine cannot do: "Fall in love, enjoy strawberries and cream, make someone fall in love with it, learn from experience, use words properly, be the subject of its own thought, have as much diversity of behavior as a man, do something really new" ("Computing Machinery" 453). Turing then addresses each of these concerns. By citing experiences such as falling in love and eating strawberries and cream, Turing places bodily experiences as central to machine intelligence. He implicitly feminizes intelligence by including emotion—falling in love and making someone (or some machine) fall in love with a machine. Thus, Turing aligns the performance of intelligence with stereotypically feminine activities. His measurement of intelligence includes feminized embodied experiences. These are the grounds upon which he defends the possibility of machine intelligence.

Consider what Turing imagined this machine could do: play chess, write poems, learn language, and sing songs. This machine, then, is doing creative, intelligent work. Some of these tasks, such as math and chess, are characterized as masculine. Turing himself was an avid chess player and almost exclusively played chess with men. At the same time, Turing suggests that the machine could do things such as write poetry and sing songs that are conventionally associated with femininity. The pursuit of these arts, especially by connecting them to the sciences, is a decidedly feminizing move. This brought considerations of taste, emotion, and pleasure into a field that has been dominated by a telos of productivity, efficiency, and rationality. The forms of thinking that are traditionally associated as masculine—mathematics, rule-based tasks, logical proofs—were tasks that Turing already knew the machine could do. To prove its intelligence, Turing needed to suggest that the machine could perform modes of thinking that have traditionally been gendered feminine. The machine's access to intelligence hangs on its ability to be gendered feminine.

One might expect Turing to use masculine terms when describing the predominantly male group of engineers, technicians, and scientists. However, he rhetorically feminizes this group with a maternal analogy:

> Suppose Mother wants Tommy to call at the cobbler's every morning on his way to school to see if her shoes are done, she can ask him afresh every morning. Alternatively, she can stick up a notice once and for all in the hall which he will see when he leaves for school . . . and also destroy the notice when he comes back if he has the shoes with him. ("Computing Machinery" 445)

In this example, the work of coding is compared to mothering. The work is analogous to feminine, nurturing labor. And the computer is her child learning to be a responsible family member. This work is done in a domestic sphere (the home) and for domestic pursuits (getting her shoes fixed). Later, Turing identifies the work of setting up the initial state of the mind (either human or machine) as a "birth" (460). These (male) mothers first birth and then raise and train their "baby" to perform tasks, learn new skills, sing songs, and write poetry.

By any standard of technical writing, Turing's is unusual, but his use of gender is particularly queer. Feminizing technologies is by no means unusual; pilots name their planes women's names. However, Turing's use of feminizing discursive practices is a criterion for intelligence, not a service or a tool. Feminine gendering is a defining quality of Turing's test of intelligence, thus making the feminization particularly important. Turing's choice to feminize computers is especially noteworthy given Brian Easlea's research that demonstrates how, when building the technology for nuclear warfare, American engineers and scientists consistently framed themselves as fathers birthing and breeding their masculine nuclear weapons. From this research of technical rhetoric, Easlea is left to conclude that "our whole culture is basically masculine in character but modern science is its cutting edge" (7). Feminist scholars and gender theory scholars have demonstrated the many ways that computers, weapons, and other technologies were gendered as masculine, thereby becoming technological extensions of masculine strength and power (Grint and Gill; Seidler; Cockburn). Contrary to this convention, Turing genders both the machine and its inventors as feminine.

Turing's rhetoric of embodiment is not just gendered but also queer on multiple levels. First, he describes gender as a performance. Therefore, gender is nothing natural, essential, or even stable. Rather, gender is flexible, an act, a cunning display of intelligence. This was especially unusual given the rigid gender roles in post-World War II England. His understanding of gender seems to also parallel some of his ideas on intelligence. Original or innate intelligence, Turing argues, is not necessary or even possible, neither for machines nor for humans: "'There is nothing new under the sun.' Who can be certain that 'original work' that he has done was not simply the growth of the seed planted in him by teaching, or the effect of following well-known general principles" ("Computing Machinery" 455). Turing reminds us that human and machine intelligences are equally shaped by education, ability, and previous experience, and even by language and culture.

The representations of gender as performative and cultural are important traces of Turing's own embodied experiences that shaped his thinking. Given the risks, he was surprisingly open, honest, and unashamed about his sexuality with friends. In the entry on Turing in the *Lesbian and Gay Studies Reader*, Steve Barbone states,

> Turing's place in homosexual studies is problematic because he neither hid nor proclaimed his sexuality and would likely wonder why it might concern anyone anyway. Perhaps his own inability to grasp why his sexuality should be of interest to others is what makes him an enigma both to those in and out of gay studies (594).

In addition, when Turing was charged with "gross indecency" after a cruising connection went very badly, he consistently declared his unrepentant attitude (Hodges 471). In doing so, he openly resisted not only the laws but also the presupposition that he had anything to be defensive about.

Turing also queers when he resists conclusive answers and explores new potentials. He invites us to relish the surprises and uncertainties of invention. Like his article "On Computable Numbers," in which he posited that mathematics was not "decidable" and would always have questions, problems, and surprises, Turing's article "Computing Machinery and Intelligence" is an invitation to enjoy the open-ended, surprising potential of computer intelligence. When arguing for the potential of machine intelligence, Turing bluntly states, "Machines take me by surprise with great frequency" (455). This capacity to surprise is all too familiar for most computer users. Turing is not offering a conclusive definition of machine intelligence. He is asking us to look for and learn from these surprises as well.

Turing wrote "Computing Machinery and Intelligence" while heady with his success and the freedom to explore a range of possibilities for machine intelligence. Turing's friend Robin Gandy read an early draft of this essay and described it as

> not so much a penetrating contribution to philosophy but as propaganda. Turing thought the time had come for philosophers and mathematicians and scientists to take seriously the fact that computers were not merely calculating engines but were capable of behavior which must be accounted as intelligent. (Copeland, *Essential Turing* 433)

Turing makes his case that philosophers and mathematicians and scientists should take machine intelligence seriously. To make this argument, he asks us to take seriously games, gender fluidity, and mothering, and to delight in the surprises that may come. Turing was less interested in marshaling conclusive, watertight arguments in defense of machine intelligence. Rather, this article is a provocation for philosophers, scientists, and theorists; they are invited to think imaginatively and creatively about the future potential for intelligent machines, which Turing saw daily.

PRIVILEGES AND VULNERABILITIES OF TURING'S QUEER TECHNÉ

This chapter locates queer rhetoric as well as Turing's capacity for resistant, surprising thinking that bends gendered expectations. Jean Bessette argues that queer rhetoric should be understood only in situ, where queer is defined by its context, situated in time, culture, and politics ("Queer Rhetoric"). I have thus far defined how Turing's queer techné resisted the standards for mathematics, writing, and theory at the time. However, that resistance should also be understood in context. Whose bodies were permitted to resist?

One of the most popular stories about Alan Turing is told and retold because it shows both his character and his importance during World War II. In 1941, Turing was working at Bletchley Park, the central location of British counterintelligence and code-breaking efforts. He felt that his work on a precursor to an early computer called a Bombe was stymied by funding and staff limitations. Bletchley Park was managed like any other aspect of the British Civil Service, as a rigid bureaucracy. Every person had a task, a role, and a place in the chain of command. Bucking the chain of command, Turing, Gordon Welchman, Hugh Alexander, and Stuart Milner-Barry wrote a letter directly to Winston Churchill:

> You will have seen that, thanks largely to the energy and foresight of Commander Travis, we have been well supplied with the "bombes" for the breaking of the German Enigma codes. We think, however, that you ought to know that this work is being held up, and in some cases is not being done at all, principally because we cannot get sufficient staff to deal with it. Our reason for writing to you direct is that for months we have done everything that we possibly can through the normal channels, and that we despair of any early improvement without your intervention. (qtd. in Hodges 277)

Churchill responded immediately, demanding that Turing's requests be met and that there be "action this day." Quickly, women from the Women's Royal Navy Service were assigned to operate the bombes. Turing had the freedom to work as he saw best with little oversight.

In this story, we certainly see Turing's drive and passion. The work of computing and the men who worked on these computers occupied a unique social space: they both benefited from and depended on bureaucratic support and financing and, at the same time, were rewarded and praised for resisting that same community's protocols. Turing benefited from a division of labor that was central to the organization of the British government. All generalists—typically women, but also lower- and middle-class men—would follow instructions, and their work was relatively interchangeable. Generalists themselves were seen as necessarily replaceable.

Describing the work of the computer operator, Turing uses the metaphor of master and slave (Hodges 367). The specialists, like Turing, were the masters who made decisions, envisioned projects, and created instructions. His assumption is that the slave merely needed to follow these instructions with careful attention to detail. Here, Turing describes women's work as slave work. A generalist's work was slave work. Slave work meant, for Turing, replaceable labor, unthinking labor, disposable labor. Buried in the foundations of digital computing, we find metaphors of slavery. And the enslaved laboring body was definitionally disposable and unthinking. Turing's very work as a "master" of this system depended on his assumption that he should benefit from the bodies of women and enslaved people. This is yet another embodied metaphor; this time it is an explicitly racist embodied metaphor. That metaphor makes his racist logics visible, as precursors to his work on digital computing.

Turing's early computers, when put to work on uncreative, administrative tasks, would also be doing women's work. In this way, Turing was empowered to benefit from both the bureaucracy, given the freedom and security it ensured, and the ability to resist its norms, conventions, and expectations. And he draws directly on racist, colonial logics to maintain that social role.

That freedom was proved an illusion when Turing was criminalized for his sexuality. David Serlin describes this era as a time that enacted nationalist pride on individual bodies and created a surge in technologies to engineer more fit and capable ones. Along with a push to engineer a more "fit" body, Serlin argues, medical technologies were used to engineer greater degrees of gender conformity. With this rise of scientific progress came scientific justifications for violent and demeaning policies toward sexual minorities. Hormone therapy, including chemical castration, was not seen at the time as a punishment. Its inventors and the judicial system praised themselves for this great scientific achievement, considered a "cure" for homosexuality (Serlin 126–37).

When Turing was arrested for "gross indecency" according to explicitly homophobic law, he was tried and found guilty. He had a choice: go to jail and lose his freedom or accept chemical hormone therapy that was considered a form of chemical castration. This "cure" was physically and psychologically painful as well as for the thousands of other gay men also punished with hormone therapy.

On the one hand, patriarchal governmental practices gave Turing the intellectual freedom for invention, supported his work, and celebrated his wartime efforts. So long as he appeared to conform to the patriarchal social norms, he benefited from male privileges. But that same government took it all away. Turing was punished for stepping outside of the masculinist, patriarchal social role. He was punished for being gay in ways both formal and informal. In the last years of his life, he lost his intellectual freedom to experiment. He lost his security clearance, his prestigious position, and the social capital that once allowed him the freedom to experiment with computers.

LOOKING FOR THE BODY WITHIN TECHNICAL WRITING

I opened this chapter with Turing's story about how he came up with his ideas for the Turing machine. He was running on a summer day, lay down in a field, and then—like a spark—he knew. I have taken his spark of inspiration and located it in a more complex embodied experience.

However, when I think of my own origin story for this book, it parallels Turing's story. I was traveling over the summer break in graduate school. I was lost. I no longer had any clue what I wanted to study for my dissertation. I just knew I wanted to study sexuality and digital media. I bought a bus ticket from Washington, DC, for a weekend in New York City. Walking through the New Museum, I came to an exhibit by multimedia artist Henrik Olesen and his collection "The Life of Alan Turing."

Olesen's portraits juxtaposed photographs of Turing with mechanical elements, quotes from Turing's archive, and computer parts, wires, and networks. The images are haunting, both clean and brutal. The body of Turing was turned into a machine and the machines merged into his body. This collection of artwork inspired my dissertation project, out of which this book has grown. I set out to explore the embodied beating hearts that enliven even the most objective, sterile discourses. I needed art in order to see Turing in a more complex light. And I needed to explore outside of my usual contexts to figure out that I had something I could contribute to scholarship on sexuality and technology.

In his glossary of scientific words, biochemist and science fiction writer Isaac Asimov defines mathematics as an abstract science with no necessary connection to material reality. He also notes that the abstract nature of mathematics is part of its appeal for Plato and other pursuers of universal truth. Evelyn Fox Keller argues that mathematics maintains a different relation to knowledge and epistemology than do sciences such as chemistry, biology, or physics (*Secrets* 39–41). These latter fields are all grounded within some material, observable reality. Mathematics, on the other hand, is separate from material reality. During the end of the nineteenth and the beginning of the twentieth century, mathematicians like David Hilbert assumed that mathematics was inherently logical, internally consistent, and ultimately solvable. This is significantly different, Keller points out, from biological sciences, which draw knowledge from material phenomena due to diversity and variability in the physical world.

Within studies of rhetoric, scholars have previously identified technical and scientific rhetoric that continues to exclude bodies.

For instance, Steven B. Katz identified expediency as the dominant ethic of technical rhetoric from Aristotle into the twentieth century. This ethic of expediency is cultivated through objective, mechanical rhetoric. Katz demonstrates this in the case of World War II German technocrats who fostered expediency in technical writing by discursively removing bodies from texts and replacing them with mechanical and numerical metaphors. In mathematics specifically, which was Turing's primary field of expertise, G. Mitchell Reyes defines the dominant discourses as a contemporary form of "Platonic Realism," in which "mathematical objects exist independently and a priori of human cognition" (475). Reyes finds that mathematics discourses continue to define themselves as opposed to or freed from the burdens of material reality, as well as rhetoric. Hence, the rhetoric of mathematics denies "precisely the Person—who is finite, lives outside of the formal mathematical code" (479). The qualities of the person that Reyes defines—finite, human, and living in the material world—these are the same qualities that feminist philosopher Genevieve Lloyd identified as associated with bodies and that opposed humanist definitions of reason.

Mathematics, as a pure science, defined itself through its freedom from application and material processes. According to William Pager, an American mathematician who contributed to computer developments in the United States, "there was a widespread belief that you turned to applied mathematics if you found the going too hard in pure mathematics" (Rees 607). And Hodges comments regarding Turing's turn to application that "such a foray into the practical world was liable to be met with patronizing jokes within the academic world" (157). But Turing solved this theoretical problem by starting in the least theoretical place—sitting at a table with a pencil and paper. Specifically, he used the kind of paper a child would write on to work through math problems. What could be simpler? Starting in this place, Turing entered the field as a relative outsider, solving a theoretical problem through concrete methods.

In this chapter, more than in others, the texts I analyze are abstract, theoretical writing. The primary texts of this chapter may be the least obviously connected to embodied experience. Yet, even in these theoretical works, Turing's technical, scientific writing demonstrates the importance of embodied rhetoric. Turing made these connections explicit. In doing so, we are reminded that the connections between knowledge and bodies are always there. The interconnections between our lives and our bodies are always there. The traces of the embodied writer are in the text to be found and felt.

Imagine what we could find if Turing had preserved drafts of either "On Computable Numbers" or "Computing Machinery and Intelligence." Would we see other embodied experiences, like a stain from a coffee mug, scribbles of frustration, or blotted out mistakes? Would we discover alternative arguments or tangents that ended in surprising places? The archives do not contain any drafts of Turing's publications. And we have no accounts about his writing process or his inventive process, his techné. We are left to imagine how his unpublished writing might offer further evidence of his embodied techné and queer thinking. However, as I show in the next chapter, letters to and from Turing and his friends suggest that his intellectual work was never too far removed from his personal life. And that his personal embodied experience was deeply intertwined with a larger queer community.

Turing's example is instructive because, unlike most mathematicians, he makes no pretense of objectivity, neutrality, or disinterest. His inventive ideas are whimsical rather than efficient: he compared testing intelligence with testing for gender, and his computers sang songs and wrote poetry. As an outlier, Turing's queer, embodied rhetoric makes visible the ways in which bodies, technologies, and discourses interact to produce new knowledge.

Although disciplined, "bodies never quite comply" (Judith Butler, *Bodies That Matter* 2), and Turing's embodied, queer rhetorics likewise do not entirely comply. Turing's queer, embodied rhetoric helps us see the epistemic power of queer techné, even in technical fields. Turing's queer techné opens questions about gender performance, gendered intelligence, and what it really means to be a human. Importantly, Turing's queer techné leaves us with more questions than answers. He leaves them open for thought, provocation, and to expand the horizon of possibility for both humans and machines. He invites readers to imagine the future possibilities for machines. He invites us to see computers with hope for their potential.

Likewise, I invite readers to see technical writing with fresh eyes, with more potential for its creativity and embodied richness. Can we move forward to study technical writing as always deeply tied to bodies and therefore to race, gender, sexuality? To do so, I invite researchers to attune themselves to the embodied techné, that process of invention that recruits our bodies and our minds, in every piece of scientific and technical writing we take up in our research. Thus far I have identified Turing's embodied rhetoric. Yet no man is an island, and Turing was seldom lonely. In the next chapter, I expand the narrative to include a community of queer friends who collaborated with Turing.

3

Queer Techné as Friendship

DARLING SWEETHEART

YOU ARE MY AVID FELLOW FEELING. MY AFFECTION CURIOUSLY CLINGS TO YOUR PASSIONATE WISH. MY LIKING YEARNS FOR YOUR HEART. YOU ARE MY WISTFUL SYMPATHY: MY TENDER LIKING.

YOURS BEAUTIFULLY

M.U.C.

This is a love letter. It was pinned to the hallway of the University of Manchester Computing Lab in 1952, and its target of affection is delightfully vague (Strachey, "'Thinking' Machine" 26) (see Figure 5). Its author was the Mark I computer, programmed by Christopher Strachey. The Mark I was capable of producing thousands of similarly awkward yet unique love letters. These letters were the first computer-generated writing. Let us first pause to reflect on the genre: love letters.

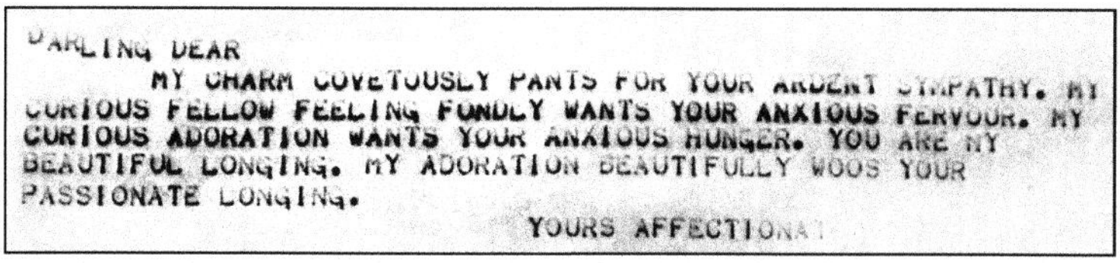
DARLING DEAR

MY CHARM COVETOUSLY PANTS FOR YOUR ARDENT SYMPATHY. MY CURIOUS FELLOW FEELING FONDLY WANTS YOUR ANXIOUS FERVOUR. MY CURIOUS ADORATION WANTS YOUR ANXIOUS HUNGER. YOU ARE MY BEAUTIFUL LONGING. MY ADORATION BEAUTIFULLY WOOS YOUR PASSIONATE LONGING.

YOURS AFFECTIONA

Figure 5: Love letter by Christopher Strachey's program and re-created by David Link. Photograph from September 30, 2012.

At the time, the University of Manchester Computing Lab was leading a series of projects with their computer, many of which were calculations for scientific research. At the same time, the researchers, including Turing and Strachey, were exploring the question, Can a machine think? Writing love letters was one of their more quixotic benchmarks of intelligence.

Strachey supported Alan Turing's vision of machine intelligence, for which they shared similar values. The intelligent machine would not simply solve problems or get work done. Their computing machine should do more; it would play and feel. Turing and Strachey, both gay men, had a playful friendship with each other and likewise with the computer, love, and the question of intelligence.

In Chapter 1, I introduce and define *queer techné*. It is a practice, an art, of nonconforming desire, a desire that may be unruly. The practice of this desiring can produce knowledge, creativity, and joy. Here, I develop that definition by locating queer techné in a broader social context of queer men through their letters to each other, starting with a letter from Strachey to Turing and including letters to and from their friends Robin Gandy and Norman Routledge.

I began the analysis of queer techné with Turing because of his importance as an inventor and historical figure. Through my archival research, I first located Turing's letters and then searched them for signs of queer community, including his connections, friendships, and collaborations with other gay men working in mathematics and digital computing. This archival research places Turing within a queer community and shows the importance of queer community for all their intellectual work. Through each letter, I analyze this group of friends as they ponder questions of what computers can or should be able to do. These collaborations are marked by playfulness, experimentation, and openness. I find that queer community was an innovative space out of which queer techné emerged. Queer world building requires an openness to making and being made outside of the social roles of hetero-patriarchal social order. In this chapter, I explore how queer friendship fosters this queer world building and, along the way, queer technology building.

I begin by mapping the community of queer friends, starting with Turing and branching out through his archive. Jacob Gaboury began to map the genealogy of queer relations in "A Queer History of Computing Parts One–Five," including Alan Turing, Ludwig Wittgenstein (Part Two), Christopher Strachey (Part Three), Robin Gandy (Part Four), Peter Landin (Part Four), and Andrew Hodges (Part Five). Gaboury traces their relationships and connections with one another, at times relations of close collaboration and at times only passing connections. Building off Gaboury's genealogy, I outline the ways in which queer friendship sustained innovative thinking, focusing on the small social friend group that appears most frequently in Turing's archive—Turing, Robin Gandy, Christopher Strachey, and Norman Routledge.

More than anything else, in the following archival analysis, I see the resonating affirmation that these men *saw* one another. And in a life dominated by the closet, the experience of being seen is a revelation. The feeling of being seen can create a space in which it is a little safer to explore and expand. The intellectual work these men did through these friendships was playful and imaginative because they were able to work within a safe space supported with intimacy and care.

By broadening to this small social network, I highlight queer embodied rhetorics animating friendships, erotics, collaborations, and, through these personal and professional relationships, invigorating technical innovations. From this we can place the digital computer in a context in which intimate relationships foster technical innovation.

QUEER COMMUNITY IN THE HISTORY OF DIGITAL COMPUTING

It can be challenging, in some ways, to identify this community as queer because these men did not identify as queer. Each of these men performed their sexuality differently: some more open, others more closeted, and others unspoken and opaque in their desire. *Gay* and *queer* would have been in use at the time, but in the records we see neither Turing nor his network of friends using these terms as identity categories. Turing identified as homosexual and refused to defend himself when he was charged with "gross indecency," thereby refusing to recognize his sexuality as criminal and in need of defense. There is relatively little firsthand documentation regarding Christopher Strachey's sexuality, but secondhand documentation from his family identifies him as homosexual. Friends and students considered Norman Routledge "flamboyant" his entire life, and he identified openly as homosexual and gay later in life. The least is known about Robin Gandy's sexuality and personal life, but biographer Andrew Hodges and Jacob Gaboury ("A Queer History of Computing: Part Four") both identify Gandy as queer, and letters between Turing and Gandy support that claim.

Additionally, we must ask how to responsibly identify queerness in a historical context that did not identify as such. How can we engage in archival research of queer lives when queerness has been systematically silenced or when these men themselves would have been guarded in writing? How can we interpret queering in the past without projecting our contemporary standards? How can we trace *queering* as a verb in their writing and the stories they narrate? I follow the work of previous scholars of queer rhetoric who theorize practices for ethical, responsible, and imaginative engagement with queer archives that have been vital for my own queer archival methodologies.

Serving as an important grounding for queer rhetorical history, Jean Bessette's "Queer Rhetoric in Situ" pairs queer theory and rhetorical analysis to effectively analyze queer rhetorical practices within historical contexts. In her article, Bessette defines queer rhetorics in historical and cultural contexts that identify both the dominant norms and what it means to queer those norms. Bessette's approach to queer rhetoric has been important for queer scholars who need to define *queer* within historical contexts. Further, Bessette's book *Retroactivism in the Lesbian Archives* is important for understanding the constructed, curated nature of archives and for theorizing lesbian identity through archival materials.

K. J. Rawson most explicitly identifies the rhetorical and political significance of archival infrastructure, metadata, and access that erase trans experience and trans people ("Rhetorical Power"). Then he offers reparative methods to recover trans communities. Further, he built the *Digital Transgender Archive*, which is a global, transhistorical collection that preserves and gives online access to transhistorical materials. But it is more than an archive. Rawson's historical activism is a "worldmaking project that merges traditional historical materials with cutting edge digital technologies" ("Transgender Worldmaking" 56).

Building on this work, Pamela VanHaitsma outlines queer methodologies that include gossip, genre analysis, and storytelling. From this work, she demonstrates her deep commitment to methodologies that both resist stable definition and encourage imaginative interpretation. Importantly, her book *Queering Romantic Engagement in the Postal Age: A Rhetorical Education* includes analysis of romantic letters that then opens an analysis of both the subject's erotic life as well as their intellectual and civic life. As I discover, the blurred boundary between desire and intellectual life also presents itself in the history of computing.

To locate and analyze queer communities in the face of erasure, we must listen differently to the archives. I am inspired by Pamela VanHaitsma's method of gossip as queer, feminist method ("Gossip" 141). Gossip is open, capacious, promiscuous in its discursive movements. Moving from one's mouth to another's ear and on again, gossip is shared, grows, and spreads. And gossip cannot be controlled by the original source. That is precisely why VanHaitsma argues that gossip is a queer rhetoric: it is not fixed and does not aspire to a single, stable truth. In addition, she argues that gossip queers due to its association with the illicit, the nonnormative. I am especially inspired by the final move in her essay in which she demonstrates queer rhetoric of gossip in practice. She "lingers over a primary artifact" because it is "marked by considerable uncertainties, but that points to still other possibilities for gossip" ("Gossip" 141). I also find myself lingering with a text, pondering and flirting with its interpretation. The poem-note that VanHaitsma lingers on opens more questions than it answers. And by posing the questions, VanHaitsma offers multiple possibilities and meanings, relations to desire, and breaks with previous conventions. She ends by asking, "What if rhetorical scholars of queer and feminist historiography flirted, however cryptically, with being 'bad eggs' as we play 'seek' and 'find' in the archives?" (145).

The erasure of queerness may be especially pronounced in archives related to the history of computing. The invention of computing was a governmental endeavor. It was funded and supported within a culture and institution in which homosexuality was illegal. It was unsafe for these men to speak their sexuality and, even if it were spoken, the institution itself had an interest in erasing queer sexuality. However, these previous scholars of queer rhetoric inspire my archival reading. I note the flirtation, playful excitement, and innuendo throughout correspondences about programming the University of Manchester computer. These letters have been saved because they contribute to the technical history of computing. At the same time, queer techné enlivens these texts. The intellectual and sexual intertwine. The letters I analyze are not new or unfamiliar to the history of computing, though they have never been analyzed in detail. The letters blur the lines between erotic and intellectual work and these blurred lines either went unseen through straight analysis or were not remarked upon.

CHRISTOPHER STRACHEY'S LETTER: QUEER FRIENDSHIP AT PLAY

Christopher Strachey is celebrated for his contributions to computer programming. He first met Turing when he was young, sometime in the late 1930s, while Turing was a young lecturer and Strachey was a student of logic and mathematics at King's College in Cambridge. Like Turing, Strachey worked in intelligence during World War II and continued to work on the same computers that Turing helped to develop after the war. He hailed from a prominent family, including well-known leaders in the arts, and he would likely have grown up in a community with more progressive notions of gender and sexuality. We have little documentation regarding Strachey's sexuality. A biographical sketch by fellow computer scientist Martin Campbell-Kelly explains that while studying at Cambridge, Strachey sought extended psychotherapy treatment after a mental health crisis: "The reason for his breakdown is obscure, although his sister supposes it may have been a coming to terms with his homosexuality. At all events, he recovered, and the problem did not manifest itself as a breakdown again" (21). After the war, Strachey worked at the National Physics Laboratory, where Turing formerly worked, and programmed the Automatic Computing Engine (ACE), which Turing designed and programmed.

I analyze one letter that Strachey sent to Alan Turing in 1951, when Strachey was thirty-five years old and working at the National Physics Lab. In this letter, Strachey writes playfully and creatively about possibilities for the computer. In doing so, I identify queer techné as both personal and intellectual desires for connection and friendship. In 1951, Turing showcased the workings of the Manchester Mark I on the BBC Radio, and it caused quite the splash. He expressed a general delight in the working of the computer, including how it could sing and play music, and how it might eventually learn to read. In the interview, Turing supposes, almost in passing, that the intelligent machine would need to be taught and trained, the same as a human child. Strachey listened to the radio program and was excited about the broad horizon of possibility that Turing imagined. In response, Strachey wrote a letter to Turing, which prompted a fascinating collaboration.

Strachey opens with "Dear Turing" and a compliment regarding Turing's radio performance. At this point, these men would certainly have known each other on a professional level, and it is likely they also knew each other personally. Strachey does not introduce himself, nor does he sound especially deferential. The letters between them are primarily professional, but there is a familiar tone as well. In the opening paragraph, he gestures toward a shared vision: "Most stimulating and, I suspect to many people provocative, but it fits extraordinarily well with what I have been thinking on the subject" (Turing Digital Archive, Strachey 1). I cannot say whether these men both knew that the other was "in the family." Given that Turing's sexuality was open among his friends, it seems reasonable to assume that these men did see a familiarity in each other beyond digital computing. The letters leave us no indication that they were anything but professional and friendly.

In the context of this uncertainty, I must read for the whispers and the allusions between these men. I read in the letters a comfort and openness to the possibilities of computing. They are dreaming together a future for their machine, which Strachey admits seems far-fetched: "This [a machine that can learn] may sound rather Utopian, but I think it, or something like it should be possible, and I think it would open the way to making a simple learning programme" (4). Throughout his letter, Strachey writes in a way that resonates with what I have previously identified as Turing's queer techné: the invention process is one of joy and experimentation, where identity and intelligence are tied, flexible, and open to interpretation.

Strachey continues to write with a particular interest in Turing's comment about how training a machine to think would be like the process of teaching a child. He relates this idea to his work on the ACE computer for a draughts program, which is considered the first computer game. Similar to checkers, draughts is a game with a limited set of rules but a vast number of possible plays. Strachey explains that he has programmed the computer to understand a set of relationships and patterns. When paired against a novice human player, his friend Anthony, whom Strachey considers "no mathematician, and would certainly never be able to discover the mathematical theory," the computer won four times in a row (3). It followed the patterns and won nearly every time. However, as Anthony played more rounds, he learned to identify new patterns and relationships. Anthony got the upper hand on the machine, which could not learn new patterns. Strachey's conclusion is that, to demonstrate real intelligence, a machine must be able to "spot new relationships when presented with unfamiliar material" (3). It would have to learn for itself through experience.

After the first two pages, Strachey's tone gains excitement. He flirts with a "glimmer of an idea" with which he has "been having some fun" (3). In describing this intellectual work, Strachey includes pleasure, surprise, play. It is just a "glimmer," but for him that hint is exciting and hopeful. This is intellectual work, but it is also about desire and the flirtation with possibilities that is a part of innovation.

Strachey explains his next stage of the draughts program. He admits that the draughts machine will eventually be outsmarted by the human. Instead of trying to pit human against machine in a purely intellectual game, Strachey programs the machine to play both an intellectual and an emotional game. He explains, "I have amused myself by making the machine impatient if its opponent is too slow, or makes mistakes, in making it lose its temper completely and refuse to play any more" (4). If the human took too long to make a move, the machine was programmed to lose its temper. If the human friend made an error, the computer would print a mocking chastisement: "I refuse to waste any more time. Go and play with a human being" (Roberts). Strachey's human friend was flustered and rushed, making poor strategic choices in the process. Personally, I am delighted by the idea of a machine that plays emotional games in order to win the game, to gain the upper hand.

While this is not an erotic or romantic letter, both men use their correspondence to participate in queer techné of computing. Avery Edenfield et al. have argued that queer practices in technical communication are ethical responses that can be "noncentralized, participatory, democratic, on the margins, ludic, harm reductionist, resistant, and accessible to aid in supporting a wide range of queer spaces, bodies, and communicative practices" (178). As is practiced by queer scholars in rhetoric and composition, Edenfield et al. identify queer technical communication not by the sexuality of the writers but by the queerness and use of the text (184). Strachey's letters, though not erotic, perform queer techné by supporting this queer friendship as well as queer space to think playfully.

Strachey continues an open, capacious, and flexible notion of what a computer can do and what constitutes intelligence. Games, play, emotions: these are what Strachey wants the computer to be able to do and express. The machine, or at least his dream for the machine, is not utilitarian, efficient. In fact, this machine does not even play fair. If the machine cannot yet learn to win by learning patterns and relationships in the game of draughts, then the machine will get the upper hand in an emotional game against the human. Winning or even learning is not necessarily the goal. Strachey is pranking his friend through the computer. And the result is creative, charming even.

The computer was not the only one mixing intelligence and emotion in its relationship with the other player. Strachey also imbues his letter with both intelligence and emotion as he is beginning to develop a closer relationship with Turing. There is joy and fun in these letters. I also read a tone of hope, that together Turing and Strachey could play with this machine and see what new surprises it might bring. Strachey ends with a compliment by way of an apology: "Please excuse such a long letter—I am quite sure you are far too busy to answer it—you must blame your talk for being too stimulating" (4).

This letter seems to have been successful in sparking that intellectual and personal relationship. They began to work more closely together. Turing sent Strachey his programming manual for the University of Manchester computer. Strachey sent it back with corrections. Strachey also used the manual to rewrite his draughts program, this time for the Manchester computer. By October 1951, Turing invited Strachey to use the University of Manchester Computing Lab time overnight. Strachey showed up with his draughts program, which, at the time, was the longest computer program ever written. He successfully programmed the Manchester Mark I to play draughts.

By August 1952, Strachey had created a program to write the first computer-generated text, which he designed as a series of love letters authored by the computer (Hodges 477–78). These love letters were awkward yet endearing. The target of affection was both nameless and genderless, addressed by quaint terms of endearment such as "Duck" and "Honey Dear." These random compositions of affection were surprisingly charming notes posted about the halls of the University of Manchester Computing Lab:

DEAR DUCK

YOU ARE MY DEVOTED LONGING: MY LOVESICK FONDNESS. MY BREATHLESS AMBITION CARES FOR YOUR DEVOTION. YOU ARE MY PRECIOUS RAPTURE: MY EROTIC TENDERNESS.

YOURS WISTFULLY
M.U.C.

This computer-generated writing was built with both Turing's random number generator program and an algorithm written by

Strachey. In his 1954 article about this program, Strachey explains that his goal was not necessarily to show the computer at its greatest technical achievement. He calls it a "simple trick," but at the same time "these tricks can lead to quite unexpected and interesting results" ("'Thinking' Machine" 27). In this article, Strachey essentially argues that computers can be intimate and creative as well, thereby making computers more relatable and fascinating to a general audience. Computer scientist David Link has since re-created this love letter generator based on Strachey's program, including the template (see Figure 6):

Generate Salutation 1 and 2,
Do this 5 times:
    Randomly generate one of the following templates:
        1. "You are my" Adjective Noun
        2. "My" Adjective(optional) Noun Adverb(optional)
            Verb, Your Adjective(optional) Noun
Generate "Your" Adverb, "MUC" (Strachey, "M.U.C Love Letter Generator")

Based on this template, the algorithm would generate unique love letters by drawing from a randomly selected word bank of salutations, adjectives, nouns, adverbs, and verbs. Link notes in particular that the sequence back and forth between reader and author pronouns *my*, *you*, and *your* heightens the sense of a relationship between the author and their beloved ("'Thinking' Machine" 25). I do not know the size of

IN SPITE of a certain impression of rather Victorian Babu, I think there is very little doubt of the intention of these letters:

Darling Sweetheart
    You are my avid fellow feeling. My affection curiously clings to your passionate wish. My liking yearns for your heart. You are my wistful sympathy: my tender liking.
                        Yours beautifully
                            M. U. C.

Honey Dear
    My sympathetic affection beautifully attracts your affectionate enthusiasm. You are my loving adoration: my breathless adoration. My fellow feeling breathlessly hopes for your dear eagerness. My lovesick adoration cherishes your avid ardour.
                        Yours wistfully
                            M. U. C.

Figure 6: Section from Christopher Strachey's article "The 'Thinking' Machine" published in *Encounter*, October 1954, pp. 25–31.

the original word bank—which included words such as *anxious, tender, beloved, passionate wish, erotic, appetite*—but it appears to be relatively small given that most of the available love letters use many of the same words arranged at random. Strachey describes the love letters himself as giving the "impression of a rather Victorian Babu" (26). A *Babu* was a term of respect for an Indian clerk in the Indian Civil Service. With this metaphor, Strachey admits that the style is a bit mechanical, that of a bureaucrat whose first language is not English. And yet, he continues, "there is very little doubt to the intent of these letters" (26). They are just that, formulaic, with word choices that are often both surprising and awkward. Nevertheless, they are vibrating with desire, affection, and erotic themes. Matt Sephton and David Link have since re-created this love letter generator online, and anyone can create their own computer-generated love letter at gingerbeardman.com/loveletter.

Jacob Gaboury has analyzed Strachey's love letter generator as a form of technologically infused "new romanticism" that produced queer objects of expression and playful misuse. Gaboury finds both surprise and affect in this program: "Therein lies the affective dimension of computational art, not in its function or utility, but in its ability to refuse function and confound planning—in short, in the unexpected" ("Darling" 26). I also find these letters surprising and delightful, though I could never imagine using them. That is what makes this program particularly queer; it refuses function. It is definitionally surprising, both that a computer would write a love letter and that the products themselves were composed with random words.

Strachey's love letter generator is a predecessor to the modern day ChatGPT and other AI-generated writing tools. As mentioned in Chapter 1, ChatGPT, released in 2023, is producing no small amount of anxiety. In the first few months of public use, it has been applied broadly, including to college essays, technical documentation, marketing language, and literary essays. I also am anxious about this AI writing precisely because of its use. It is very useful. And its functionality is expanding faster than I can keep up with, in my classroom and in my life. That functionality is also the primary difference between ChatGPT and Strachey and Turing's vision for computing intelligence. Contemporary AI writing may be too useful to even meet Turing's definition of intelligence. It is most successful when summarizing, integrating well-established knowledge, composing in formal and technical genres, and writing in standard professional English. I find it particularly interesting that ChatGPT was trained on large language models while Strachey's program drew from a limited vocabulary, words such as *desire, appetite, craving, longing, sweet.* These words strike me as particularly carnal. Strachey added words that are close to the skin, warm with the physical desire of lovers. By comparison, when I asked ChatGPT to "write a love letter," it generated the following text:

> I want you to know that I am deeply committed to making you happy and being there for you, just as you've been there for me. My love for you grows with each passing day, and I promise to nurture it, to protect it, and to let it shine brightly. I'll stand by your side through every challenge and every triumph, offering my unwavering support and love. ("write a love letter")

The program writes love in the most generic style, form, and content. By drawing on large language learning, ChatGPT composes the love letter to meet the needs of the broadest possible audience. It is stripped of the specificity and uniqueness of one lover reaching out in desire toward an absent object of affection.

Next, I asked ChatGPT to write a love letter specifically from one man to another man; it generated nearly identical text:

> I want you to know that I am committed to you and our relationship. My love for you has grown with each passing day, and I promise to nurture it, to protect it, and to let it shine brightly. I will stand by your side through all of life's challenges and triumphs, offering my unwavering support and love. ("write a love letter from a man to another man")

The current ChatGPT is unable or unwilling to compose with queer desire. Both letters are distinctly heteronormative. Desire is absent. They are free of any reference to bodies, or the desires that bodies experience. Love is defined by what Lee Edelman identified as futurity: a stable social structure that is projected into the future, most emblematically through what he refers to as the "Ponzi scheme of reproductive futurism" (4). ChatGPT did not write about children or reproduction per se, but the letters express love through promises of commitment, a future, and a life that is stable. In ChatGPT's letters, the value of love is not in the present, in desire, or in pleasure. Love is a stable family structure. The value of love is that it has a future and use: it is a safe investment. This is not a love that is joyful or a love that is playful. ChatGPT's letters are both rather sexless. Dry. By comparison, Strachey's love letters sound horny.

Given the historical context that limited their sexual and personal freedoms, these men practiced queer techné with freedom of intellect and invention that also included a strong undercurrent of desire and affection. The affection is not directly addressed between Turing and Strachey. Instead, the desire and affection are mediated through the computer and the computer-generated love letters. This mediated desire resonates with sublimated queer desire. In a context in which queer desire is necessarily concealed or spoken in whispers, these men projected their queer desire onto the computer, a kind of straightening screen that is not difficult to see through to a rich language of queer longing. These letters, both the letters Strachey wrote and those the computer wrote, are a unique location where we can see intellectual invention and personal affection woven together in code.

ROBIN GANDY'S LETTERS: NAVIGATING QUEER TECHNÉ AND COMMUNITY

Robin Gandy was a mathematician and logician who also studied mathematics at King's College Cambridge, where he met Turing at a party in 1940. Their friendship seems to have begun in earnest in 1945, when they were both assigned to work on radio decipherment systems. Gandy was Turing's closest friend. They end their letters affectionately, with "Love, Alan" and "With Love, Robin." In one letter between these close friends, I identify queer techné as Gandy navigates romantic, professional, and intellectual relationships.

Their friendship and intellectual dynamics constituted vital resources for comfort, invention, and affirmation.

In the archive and the history books, Gandy's sexuality is opaque in some ways. I have no document in which Gandy himself identifies as gay, queer, or homosexual. However, his letters with Turing contain obvious innuendo and frank discussion of their sexuality. Upon his death, the *Bulletin of Symbolic Logic* described Gandy as "a colourful and complex character who would arrive at work in motorcycle leathers, and later dominate a crowd in the nearest pub with his foghorn voice, plumes of smoke and witty anecdotes" and went on to note that his friends would particularly miss his "irreverence, erudition and mouth-watering home-made ice-cream" (Moschovakis and Yates 370). Does giving a lecture in leather chaps and dominating a conversation necessarily make one a leather daddy? I will not assume to assign a sexual identity to Gandy, but I find the question interesting. I choose to listen to those innuendos and consider the possibility of a sexual relationship or an open queer friendship. I identify Gandy within a queer community because his relationship with Turing was certainly open and accepting of queer sexuality.

The letters do not suggest an erotic relationship between the friends in any explicit way. But of course Gandy would have had good reason to conceal any romantic or physical relationship from written documentation. Given the context and the purpose of the letters, what kind of evidence should we expect from them? What kinds of unsaid knowledge and context might these men have had in mind while writing to each other? Evidence may be scarce, but queer affect resonates throughout their correspondence, in which desire for affection lies alongside intellectual connection.

In their letters, they share both personal and intellectual updates. Gandy opens his letter with a dissertation update: "Although I have not yet begun writing the dissertation, yet it all seems to be going rather well" (Turing Digital Archive, Gandy 2), which is surely a relatable bit of self-delusion for any graduate student. Gandy continues with a far more detailed and extensive report on his efforts to find a "soulmate." He first grieves the loss of his soulmates, including Turing: "Now neither Keith nor you are home

I am a little short of soul mates" (3). While I cannot say if Turing and Gandy had a romantic relationship, it seems suggestive that he refers to him as a soulmate. Gandy then reports that he had to break up with Nick [no last name listed], who he now needs to "play rather safe" around: "I couldn't carry on with Nick as before; the fact that—pity apart—this decision was easily made suggests it was right: he's going on very well, but the result is of course that we see very much less of each other when we do play rather safe; hope, believe that as a result he is getting over it all" (4). Then Gandy reports on and evaluates three different men who seem to have soulmate potential:

> David [last name spelling unclear] is too busy, and has too many friends to count as a soul mate, and Julian—who is here for another year having failed his exams is too sad. I think I have found a historian in Trinity—a German jew, but much softer than Grir H Shishaumn [spelling unclear] who will function as one; he has a passion for drawing simple geometry problems before going to sleep. (3)

In sum, Gandy has outlined relationships with two past soulmates, one heartbreak, and three potential soulmates. Although his sexuality is opaque, insofar as there are no documents of him explicitly identifying as gay, from this letter it is easy to infer queer, homosocial relations with a strong allusion to romantic relations. Importantly, these soulmates needed to be both intellectual and personally engaging. Gandy seems drawn to one man because he solves geometry problems before falling asleep. All these connections appear to be both affectionate and intellectual, and read likely erotic as well.

This notion of soulmate is not the heterosexual model of one man for one woman forever. Rather, queer techné resists squeezing queer desire into heterosexual norms. Gandy sought several intimate, soulmate relationships. These relationships seemed ripe for pleasure both intellectually and physically. Gandy's searching for soulmates does not limit him to finding "the one" but opens him up to a broad community of intimacy, pleasure, and connection.

Similarly, Gandy's relationship with Turing, one of his dearest soulmates, included personal intimacy as well as intellectual discussion of computing. After outlining a flow chart of romantic potentials, Gandy switches right back to the discussion of his dissertation and research. In the same manner that he evaluates soulmates, Gandy evaluates dissertation advisors. First, he shares the breakup: "Dr. Powell has confessed to being an inadequate supervisor and suggested I should find someone else" (5). Then he discusses a couple of options, none of whom are ideal fits for his research. For instance, "I suppose Braithwaite is technically the right person, but he is so hopelessly irrelevant" (5). Then he evaluates another possible collaborator, who was also a close friend of Turing: "Norman Routledge intends to work on logical machines: he has been given an immense reading list by Steen" (6). Gandy closes with a question written entirely in mathematical notation and a final question: "Will you be coming to Founder's Feast?" (6), an annual event for faculty, students, and alumni at their alma mater, King's College Cambridge. In these closing pages of the letter, each sentence wavers between personal friendship and intellectual connection. The evaluation of dissertation advisors mirrors the evaluation of soulmates. Gandy concludes with a mathematical question and a hope that Turing will join him at a party, all in the same paragraph. The desire for connection weaves seamlessly between math, computers, and intimate friendship.

In this letter, Gandy never explicitly requests Turing to serve in an advisory role for his dissertation. He asks only for advice in identifying a new advisor, leaving a window open for Turing to offer. Shortly after, Turing does offer to serve as his dissertation advisor. Gandy reaches out for advice and connection. And in return, Turing offers to mentor him and help as Gandy completes his dissertation research on logic and mathematics.

Turing and Gandy's relationship parallels what we see in queer friendships in a range of professional contexts. Nick Rumens traces a long history of queer friendship in professional contexts: "Friends have helped gay men to challenge restrictive heteronormative discourses that influence the roles played by family and, by implication, about what constitutes family life" (2). He first overviews a history of male friendship that has typically been defined by less intimacy, more instrumental and activity-based friends, and less frequent communication. In contrast, he then identifies gay men's friendships as resistant to this norm. Friendship for gay men serves as a place for "protection, supportive intimacy and affirmation" (36). In addition, Rumens stresses that "workplace friendships condition possibilities for gay men to explore who they are" (139). In this way, a friendship like Gandy and Turing's fosters community as well as individual identity exploration through recognition and affirmation. Although Rumens is studying a group of men nearly fifty years later and in different contexts' his research on queer men's workplace friendships documents the long-held intimate and affectionate friendships among gay men, including the friendships that supported this queer community in early computing. Working together, Turing and his friends supported one another and supported the development of innovative computing processes and technologies. Claire Sisco King and Isaac West further affirm queer kinship, which is not defined biologically and remains dynamic, because queer kinship reminds us that sexual and gender roles are performative, flexible, and negotiable. All identity is relationally dependent, in conversation, in negotiation, and co-constituted through our relations with others. The power of queer relationality lies in making visible that process of co-constitution. We lose ourselves and find our queer selves in this process of making and being made. Queer kinship roles are neither clear nor fixed. Rather, queer relations emerge and grow through our relations with queer kin.

Gandy's letter represents the ties between friendship, queer community, and mathematics. He is looking for an intimate relationship, and he has two criteria: First, he wants to have the time and attention to build a real connection. Second, he desires discussion of his work and ideas regarding his math dissertation and his future work on computing. I see in this letter a desire, and that desire is for both personal and intellectual intimacy. His desire drew him closer to some men and further from others.

LETTER TO NORMAN ROUTLEDGE:
QUEER EROTICS AND FEAR

Norman Routledge was friends with both Alan Turing and Robin Gandy. Like the other men discussed in this book, Routledge went to King's College Cambridge and studied mathematics. He attended the school after World War II, which means he would not have overlapped with Turing but did with Robin Gandy, who mentions Routledge as a classmate in his letters to Turing. Routledge also pursued his doctoral research in the footsteps of Turing, continuing to challenge Hilbert's thesis and interrogate definable sets of numbers. Given that both Routledge and Strachey worked on the ACE machine in the National Physics Lab around the same time, I imagine they were likely friends and were certainly colleagues. Unlike the other men featured in this book, Routledge was born to a lower-working-class family, and he attended Cambridge on scholarship.

Norman Routledge was a well-loved teacher and known as flamboyant by his colleagues, first at King's College Cambridge and then at Eton College. He was a member of both an organ society and a motorcycle society. His friend and former student Tam Dalyell described him this way: "Wonderfully irreverent and hugely knowledgeable, he entranced those of us who were fortunate enough to be his undergraduate friends. He was the antithesis of the dry mathematician, this bow-tied and cheerful dynamo." He carried this spirit into his teaching career, known to laugh loudly and argue with vigor. The series *Web of Stories: Life Stories of Remarkable People* interviewing Routledge features his charisma and flair for storytelling, as well as his sartorial preference for pairing bowties and leather vests. In this series and generally, Routledge openly identifies as gay. He explains, "Curiously enough, I'm only too thankful to be gay for the following reason: it was the discovery that there was something in my life that I was never going to be able to conform with that strengthened my character" ("Norman Routledge - Glad"). In the same interview, Routledge recalls a close, sustained friendship with Turing, who talked about math all the time and who was "shrieking and giggling all the time." Routledge also says, "We didn't talk about sexual matters because I don't think he knew I was gay. I knew he was gay because there was someone named Neville Johnson who took courses with me, who I was well aware was his boyfriend" ("Norman Routledge - Being Friends").

This memory fascinates me. Memories can be slippery when held against the archive. Given that all of his friends describe Routledge in explicitly queer terms, it seems unlikely that Turing would have been in the dark about his friend's sexuality. In their letters, Routledge and Turing write explicitly about gay desire and sexuality. In the video interview, Routledge recalls that Turing gave him advice about being gay: "The great part of homosexual life is that you meet a great many people of varying kind, and this is certainly true" ("Norman Routledge - Something"). Perhaps Routledge was misremembering. The letter I analyze in this chapter explicitly documents a shared knowledge of queer desire between Routledge and Turing. I can identify a queer techné in these letters as well as an allusion to queer desire. This is tricky work. The letters between these two men were some of the most explicitly erotic in the Turing Digital Archive.

In 1952, Routledge wrote to Turing and opened his letter with thanks: "What a delicious Xmas card you sent me—it was certainly the finest choirboy I've ever had—(although someone else sent me a delicious youth in pajamas peeping from behind some curtains with a charming inscription about 'here's wishing you everything you want. . . . ')" (Turing Digital Archive, Routledge 1). This letter is most remarkable insofar as it is the most explicitly erotic and homoerotic content I found in Turing's archive. It is surprising to find this level of comfortable openness. The context and allusion to "here's wishing you everything you want . . ." is one of the most explicitly erotic greetings I found in this archive. However, I do not know whether this means the two men were romantically engaged. A romantic or sexual connection seems entirely likely. To be sure, they were close friends for many years. They attended events and visited each other often, and they also worked on similar computing projects. This comment was certainly a private form of friendly, flirty banter. This may or may not have been an explicit come-on or suggest any sexual connection between them. Rather, the innuendo and flirty play signals that they had a casual, flirtatious connection over shared queer desire.

I think there is also a way to read this exchange on an ironic level. I do not have records of the cards themselves, but I am sure it would have been too dangerous to send actual gay pornography through the mail at that time. Instead, I imagine these cards were not that different from the common Hallmark cards still readily available today. In the early 1950s, these would have been prints of drawings, perhaps in the cliché style of Norman Rockwell. At a time in which sharing actual queer erotic material would have been illegal, Turing and Routledge probably appropriated the seemingly wholesome Christmas scenes and exchanged them with a queer undertone. With the context of the sender and the suggestive captions, they are practicing queer rereading that allows them to share an ironic laugh at the knowledge that representations of even Christmas scenes can be recast as unwittingly queer erotics.

After this explicitly flirtatious opening, Routledge transitions to something he is equally excited about: he was being trained to be an ACE computer operator at the National Physics Lab, the same machine Turing helped to develop. Much of the letter is concerned with the operation of the ACE machine: "My latest venture is to get ACE to do a decision procedure for Propositional Calculus" (1–2). Routledge goes on to speculate about the possible application of the "Oracle Machine," which Turing proposed in his dissertation as a random generator that never became a reality. In this letter, Routledge builds on Turing's work in two explicit ways. First, he is working on the ACE machine that Turing developed, even after Turing moved on to work on the Manchester Mark I. Second, he is exploring Turing's theoretical work on the limits of mathematics.

In the same year, in response to Routledge's letter, Turing shares updates of his own, on a less positive side: "I've now got myself into the kind of trouble that I have always considered to be quite a possibility for me, though I have unusually rated it at 10:1 against" (Turing Digital Archive, Turing 1). Weeks before this letter, Turing contacted the police to report a robbery at his home after a young man he met while cruising stole from him. While investigating the robbery, Turing himself became a suspect for breaking "gross indecency" laws. Turing refused to deny the charges.

After first reporting this personal tragedy to Routledge, Turing then attempts to make light of the situation, turning it into a story to be shared among friends: "The story of how it all came to be found out is a long and fascinating one, which I shall have to make into a short story one day, but haven't the time to tell you now" (1). However, he knows that the treatment of chemical castration will have profound effects on his body and mind, and the public outing would forever affect his career. Even before this process begins, he acknowledges, "No doubt I shall emerge from it all a different man, but quite who I've not found out" (2).

The entire letter resonates with vulnerability and restraint (see Figure 7). Turing discloses his fear to his friend in a logical form:

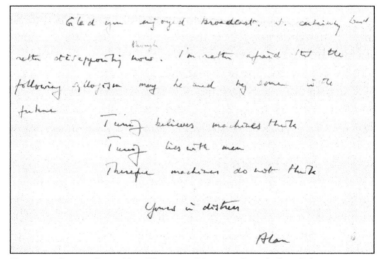

Figure 7: Letter from Alan Turing to Norman Routledge, February 1952.

I'm afraid that the following syllogism may be used by some in the future.

Turing believes machines think
Turing lies with men
Therefore machines do not think

Yours in distress,
Alan. (2)

This syllogism makes me mourn for Turing. He uses this logical form to express, in so few words, his deepest concern—that his theories of computing will be disregarded. The syllogism places his vulnerability within a logical form. Between these friends, for whom computing sealed their bond of friendship, expressing this vulnerability in a syllogism seems fitting. And in this syllogism, Turing expresses a concern that sexuality may overshadow his ideas and thinking. At the same time, he is obviously distressed at the injustice and cruelty of criminalizing his sexuality.

In this set of letters between Routledge and Turing, the queer undercurrent is significant because it shows the unique importance of queer community for these men both personally and professionally. They engage in queer techné as a flirtation and sense of play—sending sexy Christmas cards, talking about their mutual attractions. They also talk about their hope to see each other, perhaps to collaborate in the future. Even when they shift to math and computing, the element of play remains. Routledge discusses his work at the National Physics Lab, and he wonders how Turing's hypothetical Oracle Machine could be developed. Even when discussing technical, mathematical topics, these men continue to think capaciously and creatively about possibilities for computing.

More than anything else, in these letters I read a strong sense of seeing and being seen. This may be the most important thing. These men lived not just in a homophobic society that pathologized their sexuality but also under laws that punished them. The closet was a necessity. Hiding was a practice and an art of survival. That life in and around the closet means hiding, questioning, wondering if a part of you has been found out. And yet these men enjoyed between them comfort, care, and playful honesty about who they were. They flirt and discuss flirtations with others. They move between the personal, the professional, and the mathematical. There is a sense of excitement in their letters for the potentialities of the future of computing, even when their own futures are uncertain.

I want to add that queer techné is not exclusively resistance. Through resisting norms, queer techné asks us to question what is seen as normal: productive, proper, and efficient. It is given less attention, but queer techné can embrace pleasure, joy, and desire while also resisting heteronormative scripts. Sarah Ahmed urges us to hold on to resistance as a practice that also firmly holds on to the possibility of queer world building: "We can explore the strange and perverse mixtures of hope and despair, of optimism and pessimism, within forms of politics that take as a starting point a critique of the world as it is and a belief that the world can be different" (161). And I find this in the letters between these men. There is both hope and despair. I read creativity, play, and erotics alongside the very real threat of severe punishment. Even while facing trial for his sexuality, Turing writes to his friend in a syllogism. He writes in despair but with hope that, even though he has been disparaged, his theories for intelligent machines may still become a reality.

Jonathan Alexander and Jaqueline Rhodes find pleasure in the queer archive, pleasures uncovered in the texts as well as pleasure itself as a means of archival methodology. I want to search for that pleasure as well. Both special issues of *Pre/Text*, first in 1992 and again in 2018, are rich sites for queer explorations of pleasure, erotics, and joy. I also see these qualities in the technical communication of this queer community in the history of computing. Friendship, for myself and for queer communities, has long been a source of solidarity and pleasure.

Like queer sexuality and identity, queer community can be defined affirmatively, especially by how it invites capacious ways of being together. Michel Foucault in "Friendship as a Way of Life" affirms the generative potential of queer subjectivity: "Homosexuality is a historic occasion to reopen affective and relational virtualities, not so much through the intrinsic qualities of the homosexual but because the 'slantwise' position of the latter, as it were, the diagonal lines he can lay out in the social fabric, allow these virtualities to come to life" (138). In being queer, or "slantwise," queer communities can reweave the social fabric to new, capacious, affective social relations. And this openness to weaving queer social relations is exciting, generative, and uncertain. José Esteban Muñoz also theorizes an affirmation of queer friendship as a mode of world building. He practices this affirmation in his acknowledgments by writing, "Queer friendship has proven to be the condition of possibility for imagining what queerness can and should mean. The actual relational circuits I am lucky enough to find myself belonging to whet my desire for future collectivity" (ix). Queer friendship opens possibilities through the experience of seeing and being seen, trusting and being trusted, and imagining queerly what our shared lives and world building could make possible.

POST WAR CONSERVATISM AND HOMOPHOBIA

To be sure, there was an active gossip mill around the "water cooler" of early digital computing. Bletchley Park veteran Donald Michie recalled, "Bletchley had some flamboyant homosexuals" (qtd. in Gaboury, "Queer History . . . Part One"). Hodges notes that in the communities in which Turing and these other men moved, homosexuality was more or less an open secret. In high school, there were open jokes about homoerotic friendships. King's College Cambridge, where all these men attended, had a queer reputation.

The British Civil Service, with its class privilege, granted freedoms to upper-class male technocrats. At the same time, those privileges were revoked and punishments were levied for being openly gay. Both David Serlin and Hugh David have identified heightened nationalism in the postwar era tied closely to a conservative push to further ostracize nonnormative sexualities and genders. In his history of postwar use of plastic surgery and prosthetics, as well as gender hormone treatments and experiments, Serlin identifies how, after the brutalities and social changes experienced during and after World War II, there was a drive to reaffirm the strength and health of the state by reasserting the manliness and health of its citizens. Serlin documents how "psychologists and sexual scientists, moved by what they perceived to be the glandular basis of behavior, maintained that orgotherapy [estrogen that was to neutralize sexuality, which Turing was punished with] . . . was a successful program that contained the patient's tendency towards sexual transgression" (137).

Scientific expertise was deployed to punish homosexuality as a means of reinforcing the masculinity and strength of the nation. Serlin's research is specifically focused on the United States. However, similar trends can be seen in England, perhaps more so given that the landscape and cityscape continued to be scarred from years of airstrikes. Further, in his history of homosexuality in England, Hugh David documents that in the years during and after World War II, until the 1960s, there was a precipitous increase in charges for "homosexual offenses," with a peak at twenty-four times higher than in prewar years (153–54). He found that, with the return to peace time, "among homosexual men there was a palpable sense of vulnerability," and referring to the end of the wartime blackouts, "now that the lights had come on again, they felt exposed" (154). The gossip about their sexuality was a negotiation of both intimacy and risk.

LISTENING FOR QUEER FLIRTATIONS IN TECHNICAL ARCHIVES

I would like to conclude this chapter by attending to an important question. VanHaitsma's work inspires much of my own thinking about queer archival research, and when addressing questions of the sexuality of historical figures, she asks: "What kind of evidence do we expect?" ("What Can").

The question points toward an obvious truth: queerness has been hushed in the archives. At the same time, VanHaitsma's question invites us to rethink where the burden of proof lies and what counts as evidence. In queer archives, perhaps we need to listen differently. I may not be able to offer concrete evidence that Norman Routledge and Alan Turing had a sexual relationship. I do not have proof that Turing and Christopher Strachey flirted. Perhaps when Robin Gandy calls Turing one of his "soul mates" he intended a purely platonic friendship. On the other hand, how does one prove flirtation? Does the absence of "proof" of sex render these texts any less erotic or even romantic? Where in a text can one locate sexual tension? To do so, we must read generously and queerly. But also, for me as a queer person, the erotic and romantic possibilities in these texts and within these communities seem entirely likely, almost obvious.

Queer techné is an art of code switching inside and outside the closet. These men would have lived their entire lives practicing how to signal queerness to those who know how to listen, while straight listeners would hear nothing. The archives are no different. These men would have been proficient at what Michael Faris ("Queer Kinesthetic") has called kinesthetic listening, listening with and to bodies that atunes not to arguments and understanding but to desire, affect, and even the strange and excessive. This is also a model for how we can approach new technologies. Turing and Strachey sublimated their queer desire into their machine. Can we do that with ChatGPT? What would it give me? What could it open up for you?

Queer techné taught me how to listen to my body. And I practiced this queer techné in queer dance clubs. I snuck into these clubs long before I was kicked out of my religious community. Each time, I learned more about what it could mean to feel safe, and what belonging could feel like. I slid up closer to friends, charming girls with awkward energy, girls who stood to lose but were going to risk it anyway. All my life I had been taught that this kind of intimacy was dirty, wrong, sinful. But in those moments, everything felt perfect and right. Looking into eyes so close to mine, I saw myself reflected, and I saw nothing wrong. I was hiding in dark booths, but I felt seen for the first time. I built my life out of these moments of being seen. Later, in queer communities, we built spaces for my expanding desires and care for my voice. It got louder with each person willing to listen with care.

To study queerness in the archives, we attend to how we are listening. Timothy Oleksiak theorizes queer rhetorical listening:

> Queer rhetorical listening is a worldmaking practice based on the longing for kinship and community. Queer listening is a demonstration of what my consent does to me, to you, to our relationship, and the ecologies in which I, you, and our relationship exist. . . . Response and transformation. An unending commitment to be transforming. Queer listeners embrace the tension between this longing for kinship and the continuous transformations necessary for inventing meaningful responses.

My experience as a queer woman with ties to the queer community makes me sure of two things: We find our people. And our people sustain us. This can be said of any marginalized community. But queer communities are particularly defined by the chosen community. Our families of origin, childhood friends, and entire communities may reject us, but we find our people and they sustain us. That, to me, is what defines queer community. Queer community is what honed my knowledge of my own queer techné, my own embodied practice in the world that I carried with me into the archives. With this deep knowledge, I knew that Turing was not alone. I knew he had to have a community. I only had to listen for it.

Jacob Gaboury, who first sketched this queer genealogy of computing, tucks away his notes on Turing's archive in a rich footnote:

> The relevance of such an archive can be seen in the way Turing's sexual relationships found their way into his programming work, as in the case of Kjell [who had a romantic relationship with Turing], and in the fact that his ideas often survive only through his correspondence with fellow queer colleagues, as in the case of Gandy. Yet in spite of the clear relevance of personal experience to broader technological developments,

the archive of queer computing is often found to be troubling by its caretakers, who choose to bury, edit and destroy until this affective power is diminished. ("Queer History . . . Part Five")

Gaboury reminds us that if it were not for the rich connection between the sexual and the intellectual in the friendship of these men, we might never know the little we do about the queer history of computing. The archive's "caretakers," as he writes, have been careful to hide the erotic undercurrents. However, queer techné ensures that the intellectual and the sexual are inseparable. The caretakers would have had to throw out huge portions of intellectual exchange to rid this archive of its erotic current. But it was not thrown out. It sits there, perhaps troubling its caretakers. Without that tight connection between the sexual and the intellectual, we might never have been able to recover queer history at all. And this connection can be seen in every document in the Turing archive.

Robin Gandy took it upon himself to save, collect, and preserve Turing's personal documents. Gandy was a mathematician and a friend but no archivist. He wrote little notes on most documents. He wrote dates on some documents. On others he scribbled his guesses: "Must be 1940" and "Mostly about λ calcs," and he also annotated corrections in pencil. These notes and corrections can be found throughout Turing's collection, enough to make an archivist cringe. While it is certainly terrible archival practice to write corrections and notes directly on archival materials, Gandy's queer friendship ensures that queer techné is preserved and celebrated. The hand collecting, saving, and note taking is the work of a friend, not of an archivist. And this friend collecting and preserving materials is the primary hand that shapes and fills this archival collection. Without queer friendship, we might have lost this queer history of computing entirely.

Andrew Hodges should also be included in this map of queer computing. He wrote the outstanding Turing biography that includes the most exhaustive and detailed research. Hodges is also a well-respected theoretical mathematician. Like all the other men discussed in this chapter, Hodges studied mathematics at

Cambridge, though he attended from 1967 to 1971, a decade after Turing's death. While there, he learned about Turing's contributions to theoretical mathematics and computing. However, not until after Hodges also came out as a gay man and began a collaboration with one of Turing's ex-lover's current lovers did he learn about Turing's sexuality. Hodges was like the rest of the men in this community: he connected with Turing both intellectually and personally, though for Hodges these connections came through archival and interview research.

This community of queer friends supported one another, and they worked alongside, often dependent on, a community of women. Both communities have been marginalized by straight patriarchal cultural contexts. Both communities had to build friendships and communities in order to support one another. And the archives struggle to preserve the depth and richness of these communities. Yet these communities were in many ways at odds with each other. Next, I expand the narrative to include the women who worked alongside these queer men. While neither community was especially supportive of the other, they worked together, and their different modes of working contributed to the development of digital computing.

4

Embodied Techné of Women Computers

BEFORE WORLD WAR II, COMPUTERS were not the sleek, lightweight machines like the one I am typing on today. Nor were computers the clicking, whirling mammoths that filled labs in the 1950s and offices in the 1960s. In England in the 1940s, a computer was typically a white woman in her mid-twenties with a bob-style haircut that was just so fashionable at the time. A computer was a woman, or rather, "women" plural. Women would work together in large offices, each sitting at her own desk or standing in front of large Hollerith machines that stored and processed data on punch cards.

I have defined techné as a process, a craft that produces knowledge through embodied experience. Thus, while the computer as a machine dates to the late 1940s, the techné of computing as a process is a far older task. And, importantly, computing has long been both feminized labor as well as collaborative labor. Historian David Alan Grier outlines this labor history in *When Computers Were Human*. In England, the earliest national computing project began in 1767 when the *British Nautical Almanac* divided labor to work on complex calculations among many freelance workers, most of whom were women working independently at home to complete assignments. By 1831 the *British Nautical Almanac* set up a calculation office that modeled a factory, with desks of women computing their specific tasks. Here, we find that computing has long been physical, intellectual, and collaborative labor.

By the late nineteenth century, Charles Babbage formalized computing as physically divided labor, which Grier describes as "refactoring work in a way that can use workers flexibly and that gets the right skills to the right part of a production" ("Human" 14). An important shift was defining calculation not only as mental but also as physical work. Grier attributes this shift to Babbage, who "argued that since [calculation] was governed by the same economic laws as physical labor, it would be pulled into the same forms of production as had word working or pottery" ("Human" 15). Understood as a physical process—or as I would say, a techné—Babbage re-created computing as mechanical actions performed by his Analytical Machine, one of the first prototypes of a computer. However, the work of computing continued to be feminized, collaborative labor well into the twentieth century. The title "computer" referred to a woman, and computing has always been women, plural. Computing continued to be an embodied process completed in large rooms of women at desks, each with their assigned computing or analytical task.

Despite the fact that women often outnumbered men in the governmental computing labs, these women have been assigned marginal places in the history of computing. The women's names were likely removed from documents they helped to write. They were seldom named in external reports, and their importance in the lab has largely been obscured by the men's invention narratives. Women like the unidentified woman in Figure 8 would have operated the Mark I and subsequent machines as both programmers and primary operators. However, in the metadata for this image in the Computing History Museum, the photo is titled "Ferranti Mark I computer," without mentioning the fact that there is also a woman in this photo. The descriptive text details the progress on programming the computer to play chess yet does not so much as mention the presence of the woman in the photo. She becomes synonymous with the computer.

In this chapter, I locate and analyze the technical writing of women working on the Manchester Mark I, especially Cicely Popplewell, Audrey Bates, and several other women whose contributions to early digital computers have not been previously studied. As I show in Chapter 2, Turing explicitly feminized intelligence on multiple occasions. However, his openness to feminized concepts

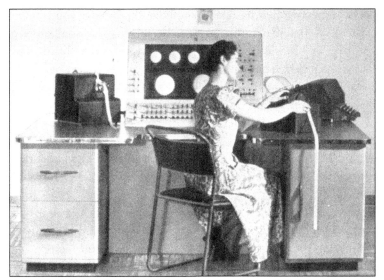

Figure 8: Unidentified woman operating the Ferranti Mark I computer, 1953.

of intelligence did not translate to respect for the intelligence of the women in his life. As Andrew Hodges wrote after an interview with Turing's assistant, Cicely Popplewell, "It was not a happy arrangement, for he never really acknowledged their right to exist" (505). The previous chapter traces the important community of queer men who supported one another in playful inventive work on early computers. These men supported each other under the threat of state-sanctioned criminalization and punishment. And yet their support of one another as sexual minorities did not extend to support women as gender minorities, nor did it remove the men from the broad culture of misogyny. Alan Turing, the community of queer men, and the women technologists all worked together, albeit worked differently, to develop digital computers. They all employed modes of embodied techné. And their different embodied experiences shaped their different contributions to digital computers.

The women's technical writing—especially everyday administrative documents such as letters, manuals, and logbooks—

documents how their particular embodied knowledge contributed to the development of early computers. While they have not received scholarly or historical attention in the way that Alan Turing and Christopher Strachey have, these women's names appear on nearly every page of the archives of the University of Manchester Archives History of Computing Collection, which documents the progress of the Manchester Mark I, the first fully programmable computers, and subsequent commercial computing models. I identify their embodied techné as a critical resource for invention and locate that techné not in individual achievement but through collective labor and collaboration.

Based on my analysis of their embodied techné, it is clear that the knowledge and expertise of these women sustained early digital computing projects in the University of Manchester Computing Lab. Their work of invention may not look like prevalent individualistic, male-dominated models of invention—and that is precisely why their embodied techné is notable. By identifying their embodied knowledge and expertise through these women's technical writing, I also seek to reimagine what innovation looks like when it includes physical practices, emotional intelligence, and the power that women leverage as administrators.

WOMEN OF THE UNIVERSITY OF
MANCHESTER COMPUTING LAB

There has been extensive research recovering the contributions of women in the history of computing, with Janet Abbate taking the lead, writing women programmers back into the history as well as studying these women's experiences as a means of documenting gender discrimination. Abbate's work, which includes both archival research as well as oral histories, reminds us that women have always been integral to the history of computing and its invention, including at the highest level of academic and technical expertise. She recovers these women's histories and their experiences as experts and innovators in early digital computation.

To this recovery effort, Mar Hicks's extensive archival research resists the narrative that a few especially tenacious women were able to break through a male-dominated industry, the narrative we see in the films *The Imitation Game* and *Hidden Figures*. Instead, they demonstrate that all computing and programming work was defined as women's work, feminized labor designed for middle-class white women. Hicks highlights the predominance of women in computing by noting that "the manufacturing workforce at IBM UK was so feminized that management measured its production in 'girl hours' rather than 'man hours' into the 1960s" (21). Women drove the computing industry in England as computer operators and programmers and even built the machines.

Hicks also identifies the British Civil Service's deliberate choice to reassign computing work from women to men as the value of computers increased and demonstrates how this sexist practice not only hurt women's opportunities but also hindered computing industries in England and stifled economic growth. From Hicks's historical research, we see the many ways in which "sexuality, the organization of labor markets, and the functioning of the economy as a whole become inextricably linked" (5). Hicks does not attempt to re-create a hero-inventor story from these women's work. They explain: "Most women in this study did not make major contributions as individuals, but they were important as a class of workers on whose shoulders was laid incredible technological responsibility with little corresponding economic or social status" (16). Rather, they demonstrate that computing labor itself was feminized and sexualized, and with that came a social context in which women became embodied, social infrastructure sustaining innovation toward computing technologies. Hicks's research on the British Civil Service parallels the time period of the University of Manchester Computing Lab. However, the different context created unique roles and opportunities for women in computing.

In the University of Manchester Computing Archives, I identify women's writing and contributions in three main places: letters, instruction sets, and logbooks. The women are not named in external reports and articles, though they likely helped to draft, type, and revise these documents. In the day-to-day writing of the University of Manchester Computing Lab, women's contributions can be found everywhere. While it is certain that many more women worked in the lab, historical accounts have identified only three women thus far—Cicely Popplewell, Audrey Bates, and Mary Lee Woods (mother of Tim Berners-Lee)—who worked in the lab in the years of digital computing after World War II. There is limited information about any of these women, and none of them is included in either Jane Abbate's or Mar Hicks's research that focuses on governmental projects. I have identified more women working as programmers or operators because the letters and logbooks also include the names of many women by last name. For instance, an entry in the 1953 logbook lists a Miss Ward as operator working through the night from midnight until 8:00 a.m. on August 12, 1953 (see Figure 9).

The absence of first names was common in the logbooks. That same page lists Miss Padfield as an operator the day before. I identify several women, including Miss Ward, Miss Padfield, Miss M. Tunnell, Miss Fletcher, Mrs. Shaw, and Miss Atkinson. I am unable to identify first names or any supporting information for these women. Letters and logbooks list last names, and women were always referred to as Miss or Mrs. Compounding the challenge of identifying these women, many of them married or remarried in the years after the war. When they changed their names, their identities in the archives were split like threads, and it is unclear which strand connects to the other. For instance, Audrey Bates married twice after WWII. To trace her career, I searched for both of her married names as well as her maiden name.

There is some documented research on Bates and Popplewell, who were both hired to assist Alan Turing in 1949. Popplewell

Figure 9: Logbook entry from August 12, 1953, signed "operated by Miss Ward" from midnight until 8:00 a.m.

graduated from Cambridge, where she studied math in the same program as Turing and his collaborators. While historical accounts of Popplewell identify her primarily as Turing's assistant, the archives show that she worked at Manchester far longer than Turing did. She held an important role programming, operating, and managing access to and terms for the computer. From his local research on the Manchester computer, Swinton writes,

> Among those with memories of the Mark I, Popplewell's stand out for emphasizing the physical work of interacting with the machine, pulling levers on the punch tape reader and running up and down stairs in the sweltering summer of 1950, as well as the emotional work of smoothing the feathers that Turing ruffled on the engineer, who had to be constantly present to manually switch the disk drive on and off every time it was used. (*Alan Turing's Manchester* 119)

Swinton also writes, "She was remembered as a universally-liked mother-figure at the Computing Service" (*Alan Turing's Manchester* 119). Popplewell was widely respected as an expert in programming and computer operation. In 1961 she traveled to Argentina as an expert to train and set up computers there, and in 1962 she published a textbook on computer programming. She held a central programming and managerial role in the Manchester University Computing Lab until around 1970, when she retired after getting married.

Audrey Bates was a Manchester local who studied math at the University of Manchester. Max Newman, head of the University of Manchester Computing Lab, recruited Bates to work in his lab to develop how to use machines to do symbolic mathematics. While working in the lab, she also earned her master's degree at the university, with Alan Turing as her mentor. After completing her MA, she continued to work in computing as a programmer. Bates was recruited to move with the Mark I when the Ferranti company expanded the project to commercialize computers in Canada. When Ferranti sold its second machine in Toronto, she moved with the machine and continued her career well into the

1970s as a systems analyst in Canada and then the United States, where she was described by a US think tank as a futurist (Swinton, *Alan Turing's Manchester* 121).

Bates's work was valued but not always attributed. Swinton explains that "when Ferranti's Vivian Bowden produced his book *Faster Than Thought* introducing electronic computers to the public, she [Bates] was a partially uncredited co-author" (*Alan Turing's Manchester* 119). Commonly, men recruited women for their experience and expertise to advise and write and then took credit for both the insights the women shared as well as their writing. Bates may have been more knowledgeable than her male colleagues about the operation and programming of these early computers because women would have had more daily experience with computer programming and operation.

I analyze the technical writing of Popplewell and Bates because their names appear most often in the archives. However, these women collaborated with several other women. This community of women collectively held the embodied techné of computer operation and programming. Their technical documents highlight how their embodied techné was critical for the invention and development of early computing. I highlight three main modes of embodied techné—physical operation, emotional experiences, and administrative power—that show how these women worked together to contribute to computing.

AUDREY BATES AND CICELY POPPLEWELL: OPERATING AS EXPERTISE

By 1948 the Manchester Small Scale Experimental Machine, which the operators called "baby," was newly in operation as a fully programmable, stored-memory computer in the University of Manchester Computing Lab. Do not let the name fool you—this baby filled an entire room, with floor-to-ceiling towers containing hundreds of vacuum tubes that lined three walls of the room. Connecting the towers was a nest of wires that buzzed and hummed overhead. At the center of this matrix of towers, switches, and wires sat a keyboard for the programmer to control the machine. The computer operated with stored data on cathode ray tubes and was read much as radar equipment would be read. This machine required a programmer's physical expertise and endurance to operate and adjust the many tubes and wires. Beyond this, operating and programming the computer required a keen attention to detail, an intimate familiarity with the complex nexus of switches and nodes.

It was a roller coaster trying to operate the computer. For instance, the engineering log on June 7, 1952, is filled with frustrations and triumphs:

1–3:35pm: pretty good.
3:35pm Disaster!
3:40–6:00pm good running
6:00pm Machine went dead.

On days like September 6, 1951, the unidentified operator writes in frustration, "Clodding intolerable, I quit!" (National Archive, "Ferranti Mark I Log Books, 1951"). These notes are not attributed to a specific operator. No matter the user, the notes illustrate that operating the computer was no simple task, reminding us that invention includes the iterative, embodied, everyday experience of computing. Computing is a practice, and that practice elicits both knowledge and affect. The women whose computing labor was the foundation of digital computing knew intimately the complex process of computing labor.

Cicely Popplewell and Audrey Bates developed expertise through an intimate, detailed, embodied experience with the Mark I; they trained toward a capacity for computing through daily use. In some cases, they were the primary users. Their bodies knew the machine, and that embodied knowledge and familiarity was vital for both the operation and the development of computing and programming. In their definition of *techné* for medical rhetorics as "experiential knowledge and embodied practices," Edwell et al. emphasize that what makes techné unique is that "the aim of techné is dynamic, arising out of the process of making. In sum, rhetorical techné is a realm of contingent knowledge that is produced in relation to context, specific communication practices,

and the rhetor" (51). Here, techné is enacted as embodiment—
the practices, experiences, and socially contingent relations that
compose embodied knowledge.

Popplewell's and Bates's embodied knowledge is recorded
primarily in the engineering logbook, of which the National Archive
for the History of Computing at the University of Manchester
holds volumes from 1951 to 1958. Women's hands are on every
page for nearly a decade. The logs are lined with notes in which
each operator would document the work done, time in operation,
and any problems or solutions. The day-to-day process of operating
the Mark I can be traced in these logs, which include both precise
technical details as well as the operator's experiential response (see
Figure 10).

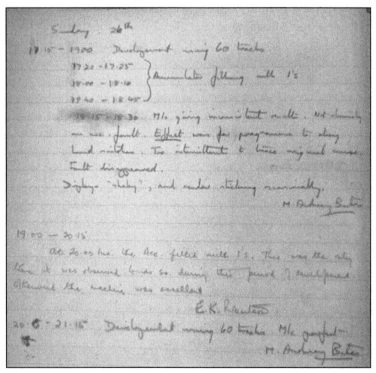

Figure 10: Two entries signed by M. Audrey Bates on Sunday, August
26, 1953.

For instance, in a logbook entry on July 13, 1953, Popplewell records her experience operating the computer from midnight until 8:00 a.m. working on a "development using 18 tracks," which was relatively high for this year. In this one line, we see Popplewell's dedication—working through the night—and her technical expertise developing an especially complex project. During this late-night stretch, she runs into "great difficulties experienced due to input," and then continues to experience "occasional difficulties" when writing the results. She reports "sporadic errors made by the machine occasionally throughout the night." In this one page, which was one of hundreds, she demonstrates her expertise in developing a program with that many tracks, indicating that she was performing a complex operation. Additionally, she needed expertise and detailed familiarity with the functioning of the machine to fix the many difficulties and errors she experienced throughout the night.

Popplewell was not just an administrator or assistant—she had technical experience and led projects just as often as the male researchers did. In a report of completed and ongoing projects in 1952, Popplewell is listed as the leader on several projects, including "inversion of matrices" and "ordinary differential equations." These are computing tasks that could be applied to nearly any scientific or commercial project (National Archive, "Summary of Work in Progress"). Popplewell was already able to program the Manchester Mark I to compute differential equations successfully for two projects: a study of binary star formation and Schrödinger's equation for the Helium atom. The report states, "These projects have resulted in two working programmes. Miss Popplewell has inverted numerous matrices of sizes ranging from 4x4 to 20x20 for outside organizations." Popplewell also wrote the vast majority of the programming library, which included hundreds of instruction sets (National Archive, "Mercury Programming Library, 1958–62"). These instruction sets were prototypes for computer programming. In addition, Popplewell is likely an unattributed writer of many of the technical documents in the University of Manchester National Archive for the History of Computing. For instance, Turing is credited with writing the first programming manual for the Mark I. However, everyone found this manual unusable and difficult to decipher. It was Popplewell who rewrote the manual into a more legible document. At the time, she would have had far more daily experience with the computer than Turing had, and her name appears in the logbook far more consistently. Her work with it and her experience as a programmer made her an expert technician and technical writer, able to compose the programming manual that was used by the operators, scientists, and engineers.

On August 4, 1953, the logbook documents Audrey Bates actively repairing the machine, not just operating and programming it. In this way, her work was far more hands-on than even programming, which was her primary expertise. In the logbook, she documents her work "soldering a thin brass cap onto lamp prode [unclear word]." She also documents her experiments with different tape options to see which functions best. There were simple days too, like June 27, 1953, when Bates recorded, "Development. Machine perfect." Bates did the work of a programmer, an analyst, a mathematician, and an engineer. Her familiarity with the computer went far beyond use. Instead, she was actively working to develop the Mark I into a more reliable, usable general-use computer.

The engineering logs also document close collaboration between these women. On July 17, 1953, we find that Miss Fletcher and Miss Woods shared the machine, which was common. On this day, Miss M. C. Woods furthered "development using about 10 tracks. Machine perfect except for one minor clod." Later that day, the log list by Miss Fletcher reads: "m/c used for production. Machine perfect except for one clod at 1.30 in store 5." These women were working from midnight until 2:00 a.m. and from 2:00 a.m. until 8:00 a.m.

The University of Manchester Computing Lab was not a governmental computing lab. Instead, it focused more on scientific research, technical innovation, and theoretical computing. In this context, computing would still have been considered men's labor. This means that some of the trends Mar Hicks identifies are not consistent with those of the University of Manchester Computing

Lab. There were more men in the lab than women. The work did not require a large team. In addition, the labor itself was coded masculine because it was research, not administration or civil service. However, while men were in leadership positions, women were still operating, programming, and working as analysts.

The embodied experiences of these women were resources for problem solving and operating the machine. Over time, they cultivated a kind of *metis*. In "Breath upon Us an Even Flame," Jay Dolmage theorizes metis, a form of embodied rhetoric that produces knowledge through embodied movement and energy. By thinking through metis, Dolmage reframes embodied rhetoric to highlight the epistemic potency that emerges from physical movement, experience, and particularity of embodied difference. Embodied knowledge is produced through life, breath, movement, and the experiences of our unique bodies living and moving in the world. *Metis* and *techné* are related terms, but techné explicitly refers to process and practice cultivated over years of repetition and informed by wisdom or knowledge. Metis animates the embodied knowledge, while techné translates embodied movement into a practice that becomes second nature in art, craft, and, in this case, computing. Popplewell and Bates honed the craft of computing while working long nights with the machine. Their embodied experiences shaped the programming, operation, and development of early computing at the University of Manchester Computing Lab. Further, because these computers and the operation manuals were the groundwork for one of the first commercially available computers developed by the electronics firm Ferranti, embodied knowledge translated into further developments for early computers.

Women's embodied techné is important because it recenters the labor and work of women whose work is often erased or seen as menial in the history of computing. Jordyn Jack has argued that everyday technical documents, rather than more scientific or abstract theoretical work, were more likely written by women, and that they are important sites of studying women's scientific contributions (*Science* 6–8). In the University of Manchester Computing Lab, much of the men's work was theoretical and scientific. Women were the primary writers of technical documents, everyday documents that shape the operation and ensure success, composed through the embodied techné of computing.

FEELING FOR THE MACHINE:
EMOTIONS THAT ANIMATE TECHNÉ

Embodied knowledge is not exclusively muscle memory or technical skill for using a computer. All embodied experiences come tied to emotional responses; movement brings feeling with it. These feelings are not tangential to invention and expertise. Rather, emotions contribute to the process of invention and collaboration to operate emerging technology. Cultural rhetorics also identifies embodiment as a key threshold concept, especially embodiment within physical, environmental, and political contexts toward social action (Cedillo, "Diversity" and "What"; Cobos et al.; Medina-López; von Petersdorff). Out of this cultural rhetorics framework, Cristina Cedillo theorizes embodiments with nuance for difference in which emotion is a key intersection of difference ("What" 2–3). She argues that nonnormative bodies have been overly determined and identified by their bodies. These bodies are then associated with emotion, thereby losing credibility in a logocentric system. And yet our emotions tell us information and how to navigate social contexts. For the women in the University of Manchester Computing Lab, emotional intelligence was a premium skill set.

Both the technical and the emotional labor of computing are written onto each page of the engineering log. As with so many technologies, the operators' relations to programming are both instrumental—wanting to get things done—as well as emotional—getting things done builds our investment, care, hope, frustration, and excitement regarding their possibility. After reporting technical details of their work, the operators and engineers also wrote a line or two about their experience with the computer. These experiences include what operation or program they were computing and an evaluation of the computer or their own personal response to the operation.

Wrong answers and errors seem to be the rule rather than the exception. In the 1953 logbook, Mrs. Tunnell writes, "Machine quite good on the whole. About 20 errors in computation occurred during this period. At one point it was found to be impossible to write anything into the accumulator but this fault cleared in a few minutes. M Tunnell." In the 1958 log, A. Kirk writes on October 16, 1958, "machine working like a lamb." But on December 28, she records, "Control regulator clodded for a few minutes. . . ." Then, just a few hours later, Kirk writes: "Wrong Answers!"

On August 26, 1953, Bates documents her work in the logbook on a Sunday to troubleshoot and run a program that included "development using 60 tracks." It sounds like a frustrating day, with the computer first "giving inconsistent results" and the inability to identify what was faulty. Then, after troubleshooting, she reports, "fault disappeared." Finally, after 8:00 p.m., she writes, "development using 60 tracks. Manchester Computer perfect."

These women included both technical details as well as their emotional responses: they record feeling satisfied, frustrated, bored, and pleased. Read together, I find that these emotional responses helped to guide their workflow. They allowed their experience and emotional responses to decide when to turn the machine off, when to take a break, and when to start from the beginning. Operating this early computer was a recursive, physical, and emotional process through which these women gained not only expertise with the machine but also intimacy. From this position of practice and experience, they successfully engineered and programmed early computers.

The logbooks and letters clearly document these women as collaborators who relied on one another for expertise and professional support. But I cannot say from the archived materials whether these women were also friends. Did they lean on each other for emotional support? Did they go to happy hours after work? The archives preserved the letters and personal documents of men, but women's personal correspondences are absent. There is no indication of their personal lives as relevant in the National Archive for the History of Computing at the University of Manchester. I do know that Popplewell and Bates shared an office in the University of Manchester Computing Lab. Perhaps they did not need to write letters. I imagine them gossiping between meetings and complaining about a clod in the computer between operating shifts. Bates was eight years older. When I use my imagination, I hope that Bates offered Popplewell dating advice. Or maybe they complained about their dates, humoring the men with their time when they had better things to do. I hope they complained about the computer and called the computer their girl. Maybe they took their shoes off in the lab on summer days and drank tea midday. They must have relied on each other for advice with programming or analysis. I imagine these friendships because I know my own experience of professional success has been shaped by female friendship. I was the only woman in my PhD program cohort. I would not have survived without the friendship of women in the department. We talked about work, books, sex, writing, children. We gave each other dating advice and shared the details. And we always complained about men whose attention we had to humor. These are the conversations that supported me as a professional and as a person. I hope the women who are recorded in the Manchester Computing logbook enjoyed the same support.

I can envision their friendship. I cannot locate it in the archive. Even in conjecture, I hope that in this professional environment working primarily with men, many of whom were patronizing at best and often misogynistic, these women found some comfort in one another while collaborating.

CICELY POPPLEWELL AND THE ADMINISTRATIVE LABOR OF COMPUTING

The University of Manchester Computing Lab was a university-based research site with different goals and social structures, and its divisions of labor were less rigid than those of the British Civil Service that Hicks studies. Because of this, the Manchester archives are a fascinating place for locating women's contributions to the history of computing. The lab and its directors had more intellectual and creative freedom. They were working on computing for tasks that were scientific, experimental, and commercial. Sometimes it seems as though they were programming the computer out of pure experiment and curiosity: What could a mechanical mind do?

What does it mean to think? This was also a university-sponsored venture that grew into a commercial enterprise, led by the Ferranti company. Hence, the University of Manchester Computing Lab was a unique space for experimentation and exploration of what a computer could do.

In addition, the roles of women seemed to be different. There were fewer women at Manchester than women working for the British Civil Service. Some of the women in the University of Manchester Computing Lab were hired as assistants. However, in these assistant positions, they also earned advanced degrees, led their own experiments, and gained valuable expertise.

In addition, women played a gatekeeping role, with power to negotiate access to the computer. This was especially true for Cicely Popplewell. This role can primarily be seen in the National Archive for the History of Computing, which contains many letters to and from Popplewell. In the letters, she negotiated prices and time on the computer, and she helped other scientists and those in the industry plan their computing projects. Popplewell wrote detailed instructions for programming and operating the computer.

The fact that women were assigned most of the administrative and emotional labor will come as no surprise to most of my women readers. Scheduling meetings, taking notes, reserving rooms: these tasks seem to unevenly fall on women's shoulders. However, I must emphasize that this work was not exclusively supportive. Rather, the administrative labor was an important gatekeeping function because it positioned these women with some power to grant and regulate access.

In a letter from August 22, 1961, Popplewell responds to a Professor Evans from the Department of Geology at Nottingham University who requested the Mercury machine in use at that time (National Archive, "Correspondence with users of Mercury, Nottingham University"). She responds politely with a greeting of thanks. Then she assures Evans that "we already do a considerable amount of work for the Physics and Engineering departments at Nottingham University" in a gesture of assurance to demonstrate competence before setting the hourly rate. In the subsequent paragraph, she begins to advise and direct the work: "If your programme is untested I would suggest that you let us do a short test run of about 5 minutes before embarking on a 30 minutes production run." In this sentence, Popplewell administers the timing and procedure for the use of the computer. She recommends best practices that will dictate the pace and schedule for the work. She continues to direct the form and guidelines for the project:

> I am enclosing some copies of the instructions sheet which would accompany the programme. One of these, together with the tape and a print-out of the programme, should be sent to Mrs. D. Atkinson of this laboratory who operates our Computing Service.

Popplewell is doing the work of instructing and standardizing the instructions for clients. These instructions are then used as tools that inform how the programme is written. Then Popplewell directs Evans to another woman, Mrs. D. Atkinson. Even in administrative roles, these women collaborated and leaned on each other as experts.

Popplewell and other women in this computing lab defended and supported the advice and work of other women, thereby creating a community of women collaborating and supporting one another. Together, with their expertise and their collaboration, they held power in the lab. In a letter from August 25, 1961, responding to a request for time on the machine from Mr. Davey of the Aerodynamics Division of the National Physics Lab, Popplewell advises and sets terms: "The first point I want to clear up is whether the programmes you propose to run are fully tested. If not, then I think you should come prepared to do some preliminary development and testing during the Maths Department's time on Monday evening" (National Archive, "Miscellaneous correspondence, 1958–62"). In the next paragraph, she says, "As Miss Shaw very rightly pointed out, the demand for machine time is extremely heavy and it is impossible to say exactly what time we shall be able to give you until we make up that week's time table." Then, referring to a previous conversation with Mrs. Atkinson, Popplewell sets the financial terms: "Mrs. Atkinson tells me that she has done a fair amount of work for you recently and that you seem to be worried about being charged for the time. As this is work for your Thesis [sic] there is no question of payment." In this one letter, we see Popplewell mediating between the machine and Mr. Davey. In addition, we see her collaborating with and supporting the other women operators, Mrs. Atkinson and Miss Shaw.

In a series of letters in 1960 between Popplewell and Mr. Adams, written on behalf of Atomic Power Construction Limited, Popplewell sets terms, negotiates price multiple times, and sends instructions (National Archive, "Miscellaneous correspondence, 1958–62"). More than that, she has to negotiate these terms according to the needs of each project and client. On December 8, 1960, after four letters sent back and forth, Popplewell writes: "Thank you for your letter of the 7th December. I am afraid that there are still one or two points in Clause 4 which we cannot accept." After correcting the language and its presuppositions about how much time a task will take, Popplewell sends Adams corrected language for the "Clause 4" writing: "I would suggest that Clause 4 should read as follows," and then provides exact language for the contract.

These women also troubleshoot technical problems via letter. They advise on programming, operation, and timing, and offer advice when the machine does not work. Their embodied knowledge through practice made them experts, and the male scientists depended on that expertise. The men they correspond with appear to recognize their relative power and treat them with more than just professional respect, speaking to the women instead with gratitude and graciousness. In a letter on December 1, 1960, Mr. Adams writes to Popplewell by addressing her as "Madam" and then finalizing their negotiation of terms: "I should take this opportunity of thanking you for your cooperation in this matter. Yours faithfully" (National Archive, "Miscellaneous correspondence, 1958–62"). These words of cordial thanks are found throughout the archive.

The women's labor was equal parts technical expertise and social negotiation. Men could work solo and ruffle feathers with fewer consequences, as Turing often did. But, at every stage of the process, these women collaborated with one another, with their male supervisors, and with men who were requesting time to use the Mark I. In the letters, they often refer to other women and rely on their expertise. Their work at social negotiation facilitated work with the computer.

5

Conclusion: Queer Techné as Archival Methodology

I ENTERED THE NATIONAL ARCHIVE FOR the History of Computing at the University of Manchester expecting that queer voices had been silenced. Among scholars of queer rhetoric and writing, we often assume that bureaucratic and institutionalized archives have erased queerness. This could have been done by archivists failing to identify queer identities in the metadata (Rawson, "Accessing Transgender" and "Rhetorical Power"). Other times it was historians whose heteronormative assumptions prevented them from seeing the queerness that was archived, often describing queer desire as "intimate friendship." So I had assumed the official, technical archives of the history of computing would have erased queer sexuality.

But what I found was a resounding queer desire throughout the archive. In letters and programming notes related to Alan Turing, I found flirtations. I found innuendo. And most important, I found a close-knit queer community. Some of these men were lovers. Some were friends. All of them shared a playful queer desire to explore the possibilities for thinking machines. This is archival abundance. This is queer abundance.

But of course, this discovery was not entirely a surprise. When I was twenty, I was kicked out of the conservative community I was raised in. As I mention in Chapter 1, I was raised as a Jehovah's Witness. The congregation Elders found out that I was sleeping with my friends, young men and women, as well as other Witnesses and worldly people. They pulled me into the conference room. They offered me the opportunity to repent. I refused. I had nothing to repent for. I was already learning the pride of queer community. I was excommunicated from my family, my friends, and my entire community. In their place, I found queer community. I had been erased from my family and community, but I learned to rebuild with abundant joy. My queer community sustained me then, as it does now. Queer folks know how to find our chosen family, and Alan Turing was no exception. How might our methodologies change if we assumed queer abundance rather than silence? How might our writing expand with queer abundance?

Queer techné offers a way of looking at technical and professional communication for embodied knowledge and shows how gender and sexuality are embodied differences that can enrich and enliven technical work and invention. Toward that end, I offer an intimate portrait of technical communication. The archival materials I analyze feature emotions, friendship, play, and affection. The men and women analyzed here performed embodied and queer rhetorics that were vital for the early invention of digital computers, as well as for early experiments and explorations into what a thinking machine could do.

In addition, I also performed my own queer techné in the analysis of these texts. I bring my embodied practice into the archives with me. My own well-worn practices of queer embodied knowledge inform the questions I ask and the texts I focus on, and thus they frame my analysis. Therefore, queer techné also animates my knowledge production, playfully, experimentally, and with care for intimacy and friendship. I search the archives for traces of these embodied experiences and for the moments that make up these peoples' stories. To these peoples' stories, or at least the portion of them that has been documented and archived, I bring my own personal embodied experiences as a lens for analysis. I also practice strategic contemplation by locating myself in relation to the texts: I identify with my own presuppositions, blind spots, and values that shape what and how I see (Royster and Kirsch). I am a queer, white woman. I know a thing or two about the violence that is played out on queer bodies and on women's bodies and about our erasure.

TRACING QUEER TECHNÉ: FROM PERSONAL EXPERIENCE TOWARD COMMUNITY CARE

I started this project with Turing. His life stands out as one particularly acute case in which queer techné is signaled in both his technical writing and his innovative thinking. Originally, I grasped onto his story because I needed a character whose story I could look to for hope of queerness as a resource. In the first chapter of this book, I write that we need queer stories. I write that we need both stories of queer people and stories that are themselves queer. These stories are vital for queer futures. As queer historian Heather Love writes, "By including queer figures from the past in a positive genealogy of gay identity, we make good on their suffering, transforming their shame into pride after the fact" (32). Turing's story was the first queer life I found in the history of computing. And from his experience and his writing, I can tell a queer story of a life that was driven by a desire for more—more play, more connection, more ways of being and knowing. His character held out hope for me that, even in the most repressive communities, queerness is not a burden. It was his strength. His queer thinking, his playful imagination, and his openness to possibility all enabled his innovative thinking on computing.

My archival methodology began with an affirmation of Turing and his queer techné. When I placed queer epistemologies as a central frame for archival analysis, I wanted to enter these archives and locate his queerness not as an anecdote of another queer life ended tragically as a casualty of compulsory heterosexuality. To be sure, his life ended tragically due to homophobic state violence. Despite this, his writing and his life also highlight that queerness, for Turing, could be generative, inventive, and even joyful.

Alan Turing's unique embodied experience also became a central location where I identify embodied knowledge. In his early article on the problem of decidability in which he first proposes the famous Turing machine, he grounds his thinking in his physical experience of working out calculations. This embodied experience, which was often women's work but also would have been his own experience while a student of mathematics, became the theoretical grounding on which he proposes a kind of digital computer. This was hypothetical at the time, of course. But this line of embodied thinking also foregrounded his theoretical innovations on the limits and possibilities of mathematics. Importantly, I also use Turing's writing as a place to identify embodied techné, and I then extend that to develop a more specifically queer techné.

I knew that Turing could not have been alone. By locating queer techné in the relationships between Turing and several queer men, I locate queer techné as a social practice of queer community and friendship. As bell hooks reminds us, the definition of queerness is to be at odds with the world, "queer not as being about who you're having sex with—that can be a dimension of it—but queer as being about the self that is at odds with everything around it and has to invent and create and find a place to speak and to thrive and to live" ("Are You"). Queerness is simultaneously about resistance to the world and the will to invent, create, and live. This invention and creation can only be sustained with and for queer community. Queer is a practice we do together.

With Gaboury's series "A Queer History of Computing, Parts One–Five" in *Rhizome* as a starting place, I began with Turing and looked for as many queer connections in his life as I could identify in the archives. Chapter 3 traces a network of four men who either openly identified as homosexual or whose archival materials indicate their queer sexuality. In their collection of letters, I identify queer techné as a social practice in which friendship supports desire and longing. At times, that desire is sexual or romantic. At other times, that desire is intellectual, exploring the possibilities of digital computing. And in some cases, the desire weaves between erotic and intellectual engagement. Importantly, I identify queer techné in friendship and joy, which become the animating traits that make it safe for this community of men to share intimacy as well as professional experimentation.

Chapter 3 was the most challenging to research and the most rewarding in which to lose myself in the process of discovery. There are several movies about Turing, all of which present him as a solitary, isolated character, the lone gay man in a hetero world. In the most recent (2014) biopic about him, *The Imitation Game*, Turing is depicted wasting away, isolated at home with only a computer for companionship. These inaccurate narratives sell because straight audiences feel more comfortable with lonely, sexless gay characters. The radical potential of queer community is thus neutered.

I did not buy this narrative, of course. Perhaps this was a hope of mine. I hoped Turing was not as alone and sexless as he appeared. And all my archival and secondary research supported that hoped-for narrative. Queerness brought me to a chosen family. Queer practices brought me out of shame and created space for myself, my pleasure, and my desire. More than resistance or struggle or marginalization, I feel that queerness brought me joy, play, and community. But queerness is also something I know deeply. In my own queer embodied experience, I know we find our people. In this way, queer family has become a queer archival methodology for me. My own experience with queer family made me sure that Turing was not isolated nor was he joyless. Equipped with this queer techné, I found queer community in the archives just as I had in life.

Techné begins with embodiment. While I do begin with the embodied experience of queer community, the historical reality is that the embodied knowledge of women forms the groundwork of computing. Their embodied labor was the prototype for digital computing. Women like Cicely Popplewell and Audrey Bates had expertise, grounded in their embodied practices of computing. And that expertise informed their ability to contribute to early computer science and computer programming generally. Histories of computers have long documented women's labors as important for computing industries. However, techné is never rote practice or unintellectual habits. And neither were these women mere rote laborers. They held graduate degrees in mathematics. They contributed to theoretical knowledge on computing and innovated the early models of computer programming. Their embodied techné was learned through practice, honed through theoretical expertise, and turned into shared knowledge through their technical writing.

I related to these women from my own embodied experiences. Any woman alive then or now knows the experience of being talked down to, having our work dismissed as less serious or consequential.

Men explain things to all of us. I also entered these archives as a woman who knew that women's work must have been more than assistant tasks and rote practice. What I found was in fact women with both practical and theoretical expertise. I was most impressed with their writing. Assigned with much of the technical writing, women were both performing the computing operations and compositing that knowledge into instruction sets, programming manuals, and, by extension, some of the earliest contributions to computer programming.

My archival research affirms their work and highlights that feminizing labor did not cut women out of the computing industry. The feminized labor of operation and writing made their work central and meant their hands were seen on nearly every document in the National Archive for the History of Computing at the University of Manchester. In a personal essay, "My Body Is an Archive," I write about my own embodied experience being erased from personal archives and family. That embodied experience of erasure is a trauma that marks my body and mind. I carried this experience, and so many others that women have on a day-to-day basis, into the archives with me, and this informed my questions regarding how women's work would appear in the archive, in what genres. I wanted to see how these women maintained space for themselves in this male-dominated space. And I was curious to see whether I would find signs that they might have also held space for each other.

I needed to tell these queer stories. I needed to first affirm these queer stories. I needed to uncover the importance of women, moving them out of the margins and into the center of the narrative. We need more of these stories because they remind us that we are not so different. We are not so rare. Queer communities have supported and loved one another, with joy and playfulness. Women have collaborated. They worked hard. They solved problems. And they were the bulk of the labor force in computing until the 1980s. When I recover and celebrate these stories, I correct a historic erasure. When I began this project, I did not realize how much I needed it on a personal level. I first had to affirm and celebrate Turing's queerness. In doing so, I learned to affirm and celebrate my own. I first had to recover these women's labor. I learned to value my own labor. I began writing about these communities because I saw myself reflected in these people. Along the way, I learned that I needed to tell my own story. These women and men revealed in the archives taught me how much their stories matter. They also taught me that my stories matter, so I integrate my own queer embodied narratives throughout their stories.

More than that, the process of writing this book emboldened me to write my own story. Moving forward, I will continue to recover stories from the past. More and more, those stories are my own embodied experiences, my loves, and the friends who have become family. In that way, this research resonates with the queer optimism that Gavin Johnson offers as a way for rhetoricians to think relationally between subject and object, being and doing. Johnson concludes with a call for inventive queer rhetorics: "Queer optimism isn't about finding happiness within neoliberal futures but rather a call for composing inventive ways to live (not just survive) in the present. Queer optimism is acting, not waiting to be acted upon" (428). I have woven my personal stories into this queer historical exploration to show my own queer desire that animates the production of this analysis and narrative. These embodied experiences taught me how to read and understand queer texts, and they allowed me to imagine new ways of living and loving.

CULTIVATING INTIMACY WITHIN ARCHIVES

Queer techné is the practice that has informed my archival research, and queer friendship is the condition of possibility on which this archive exists. Robin Gandy, Turing's close friend, is the man who saved, organized, and preserved many of Turing's letters. In his will, Turing left all of his manuscripts and letters in Gandy's care. He entrusted his estate to P. N. (Nick) Furbank, a literary scholar who was Turing's longtime friend and, more briefly, a romantic partner. Queer friendship quite literally saved this queer history. However, Gandy's hand did more than save the materials. He also corrected errors, added dates, and wrote notes about location. Gandy's handwriting is on many of the documents, especially correspondences.

In this queer archival history, in which historical materials are passed between friends and lovers, altered, saved, and perhaps removed, I am reminded of the queer world making that Lauren Berlant and Michael Warner theorize in "Sex in Public." This is a world building that has space for queer capaciousness: "a space of entrances, exits, unsystematized lines of acquaintance, projected horizons, typifying examples, alternate routes, blockages" (558). K. J. Rawson extends this queer world making to locate transgender world making within online archives ("Transgender Worldmaking"). I find all three of the examples that Rawson discusses to be inspiring, and what they have in common is queer folks caring for the histories, words, and lives of queer folks. This is what I also see in the Turing Digital Archive: queer folks created the possibility of a history of queer computing by saving, caring about, and sharing the archival materials of Turing as well as his queer community broadly. The archive is now institutionalized and maintained by King's College Cambridge, yet much of the materials as well as the easy digital accessibility continue this legacy of queer world building.

I question whether there are other ways that queer friendship influenced the collection, other locations where Gandy's and Furbank's hands may have shaped the queer archive. And by extension, how might their work as friends collecting Turing's materials shape what we are able to know about this moment in the history of computing? Whenever we do research in archives, we must ask: What is missing? What are the gaps? As I looked through the archives, I noted a dearth of explicitly erotic or romantic content. There are no love letters and little sexually explicit content. However, Turing had a long-term relationship with Neville Johnson, a graduate student in mathematics at Cambridge at the same time as Norman Routledge and while Turing was in Manchester. The archive includes Routledge's letters but none from Johnson. It is also clear that Johnson and Turing collaborated, given that his name appears in the University of Manchester Computing logbook. Even after he was convicted, Turing continued to develop romantic relationships, one with Kjell Carlson, whom he met during a holiday in Norway. Both men were mathematicians who worked in computing. I am left to wonder: Where are the letters to and from Turing's partners, Neville Johson and Kjell Carlson? Would they have also intertwined erotic and technical communication? Turing later named a program Kjell, suggesting their relationship was both personally and intellectually stimulating.

The traditional reading of this erasure is to assume that it was a violent erasure of queer history at the hands of an archivist who found the material distasteful or inappropriate for preservation. I am sure that did often happen. But there is another possibility as well. Perhaps Turing removed the letters for his own privacy or the privacy of his partners. Perhaps Gandy never turned over the more erotic letters. Perhaps Furbank kept this portion of Turing's life in his own private care. In this instance, it may be that these men were not erasing Turing's sexuality; queer friendship led them to preserve Turing's privacy. Erasure might have been an act of care, the intimacy of their friendship more valuable than the representation of their friendship.

Technical and professional communication often centers usability, purpose and outcomes, and efficiency. In contrast, this book affirms the play, affect, desire, and even erotics of technical and professional communication. Play we have theorized. It can be made productive, professional, educational. Certainly in this book, play can be those things. But most of the time, for Turing and his friends, play led to failure by an external standard. I like to imagine that Turing would not have found ChatGPT especially interesting. In 1948, Turing wrote, "If a machine is expected to be infallible, it cannot also be intelligent" ("Intelligent Machinery" 394). ChatGPT seems to be too useful, too widely applicable. It will only continue to improve, and with each version of ChatGPT closer to infallibility, it takes a step further from Turing's definition of intelligence. Turing's definition of intelligence did not become a reality. Strachey's computer program never generated any commercial success. That, however, was not the purpose of their play. Rather, their playful reimagining connected them to each other and channeled their desire to imagine potentials for other ways of being through the computer.

Erotics in technical and professional communication are harder to imagine and harder still to be integrated into practice. There are only hints at erotics in the archives. The queer community did not put their erotic desires into writing, perhaps because the risk was too great. Or perhaps they did, and that writing was not preserved. Nevertheless, I locate undercurrents of desire and erotics through queer techné. But queerness is not reducible to erotics, sexuality, and desire. It is much more than that. At the same time, I refuse to eradicate sex from sexuality. Tracing my finger along the text looking for the pulse of desire beneath their words, I found that the minds and bodies who conceived of and built our first computers imbued their work with desire, care, and community.

NOTES

1. For a full discussion of ancient uses of techné, especially its pre-Platonic, Platonic Aristotelian roots, see Angier's *Techné in Aristotle's Ethics: Crafting the Moral Life*.
2. For arguments against the common narrative that Turing was a "founding father" of digital computers, see Thomas Haigh's "Actually, Turing Did Not Invent the Computer" and Maarten Bullynck et al. in "Why Did Computer Science Make a Hero Out of Turing?," both published in *Communications of the Association for Computing Machinery*.
3. The Halting Problem is a computability theory that asks, given an arbitrary computer program and an input, will the program come to a conclusion, or will it run forever? Turing proved that there could be no general algorithm that would complete the calculation for all possible programs.

WORKS CITED

Abbate, Janet. *Recoding Gender: Women's Changing Participation in Computing*. MIT P, 2017.

Agar, Jon. *Turing and the Universal Machine: The Making of the Modern Computer*. Icon Books, 2017.

Ahmed, Sara. "Happy Futures, Perhaps." *Queer Times, Queer Becomings*, edited by E. L. McCallum and Mikko Tuhkanen, State U of New York P, 2011, pp. 159–79.

Alexander, Jonathan. "Materiality, Queerness, and a Theory of Desire for Writing Studies." *College English*, vol. 83, no. 1, 2020, pp. 7–41.

Alexander, Jonathan, and Jacqueline Rhodes. "Queer: An Impossible Subject for Composition." *JAC*, vol. 31, no. 1/2, 2011, pp. 177–206.

———. "Queer Rhetoric and the Pleasures of the Archive." *Enculturation*, 2012, enculturation.net/queer-rhetoric-and-the-pleasures-of-the-archive.

Angier, Tom. *Technē in Aristotle's Ethics: Crafting the Moral Life*. Bloomsbury Continuum Publishing, 2010.

Arola, Kristin L., and Anne Frances Wysocki, editors. *Composing(Media) = Composing(Embodiment): Bodies, Technologies, Writing, the Teaching of Writing*. UP of Colorado, 2012.

Asimov, Isaac. *Words of Science, and the History behind Them*. Houghton Mifflin, 1959.

Atwill, Janet, and Janice Lauer. "Refiguring Rhetoric: Aristotle's Concept of Techne." *Discourse Studies in Honor of James L. Kinneavy*, edited by Rosalind J. Gabin, Scripta Humanistica, 1995, pp. 25–40.

Barbone, Steve. "Alan Mathison Turing (1912–54)." *Reader's Guide to Lesbian and Gay Studies*. Edited by Timothy F. Murphy, Fitzroy Dearborn Publishers, 2000.

Berlant, Lauren, and Michael Warner. "Sex in Public." *Critical Inquiry*, vol. 24, no. 2, 1998, pp. 547–66.

Bessette, Jean. "Queer Rhetoric in Situ." *Rhetoric Review*, vol. 35, no. 2, 2016, pp. 148–64. *Taylor & Francis Online*, doi:10.1080/07350198.2016.1142851.

————. *Retroactivism in the Lesbian Archives: Composing Pasts and Futures.* Southern Illinois UP, 2017.

Bolter, J. David. *Turing's Man: Western Culture in the Computer Age.* U of North Carolina P, 1984.

Booher, Amanda K., and Julie Jung. *Feminist Rhetorical Science Studies: Human Bodies, Posthumanist Worlds.* Southern Illinois UP, 2018.

Bratta, Phil, and Malea Powell. "Introduction to the Special Issue: Entering the Cultural Rhetorics Conversations." *Enculturation*, vol. 21, 2016, enculturation.net/entering-the-cultural-rhetorics-conversations.

brown, adrienne maree. *Pleasure Activism: The Politics of Feeling Good.* AK Press, 2019.

Bullynck, Maarten, et al. "Why Did Computer Science Make a Hero Out of Turing?" *Communications of the ACM*, vol. 58, no. 3, Mar. 2015, pp. 37–39. *ACM Digital Library*, doi:10.1145/2658985.

Butler, Janine. "Embodied Captions in Multimodal Pedagogies." *Composition Forum*, vol. 39, 2018. *ERIC*, eric.ed.gov/?id=EJ1188981.

Butler, Judith. *Bodies That Matter: On the Discursive Limits of "Sex."* Routledge, 1993.

————. "Performative Acts and Gender Constitution: An Essay in Phenomenology and Feminist Theory." *Feminist Theory Reader*, edited by Carole McCann et al., 5th ed., Routledge, 2020, pp. 353–61.

Campbell-Kelly, Martin. "Christopher Strachey, 1916–1975: A Biographical Note." *IEEE Annals of the History of Computing*, vol. 7, no. 01, 1985, pp. 19–42. *IEEE Xplore*, doi:10.1109/MAHC.1985.10001.

Cedillo, Christina V. "Diversity, Technology, and Composition: Honoring Students' Multimodal Home Places." *Present Tense*, vol. 6, no. 2, 2017, www.presenttensejournal.org/volume-6/diversity-technology-and-composition-honoring-students-multimodal-home-places/.

————. "What Does It Mean to Move? Race, Disability, and Critical Embodiment Pedagogy." *Composition Forum*, vol. 39, 2018. *ERIC*, eric.ed.gov/?id=EJ1188979.

Cedillo, Christina V., and Phil Bratta. "Relating Our Experiences: The Practice of Positionality Stories in Student-Centered Pedagogy." *College Composition and Communication*, vol. 71, no. 2, 2019, pp. 215–40.

Chun, Wendy Hui Kyong. *Programmed Visions: Software and Memory.* MIT P, 2011.

Clinton, Alan. "The Code That Dare Not Speak Its Name: Ashbery-Turing-Roussel." *Lit: Literature Interpretation Theory*, vol. 19, no. 2, 2008, pp. 214–29. *Taylor & Francis Online*, doi:10.1080/1043 6920802107674.

Cobos, Casie, et al. "Interfacing Cultural Rhetorics: A History and a Call." *Rhetoric Review*, vol. 37, no. 2, Mar. 2018, pp. 139–54. *Taylor & Francis Online*, doi:10.1080/07350198.2018.1424470.

Cockburn, Cynthia. "The Circuit of Technology: Gender, Identity and Power." *Consuming Technologies: Media and Information in Domestic Spaces*, edited by Roger Silverstone and Eric Hirsch, Routledge, 2003, pp. 33–42.

Copeland, B. Jack, editor. *The Essential Turing*. Oxford UP, 2004.

———. "Narrow versus Wide Mechanism: Including a Re-Examination of Turing's Views on the Mind-Machine Issue." *The Journal of Philosophy*, vol. 97, no. 1, 2000, pp. 5–32. *ResearchGate*, doi:10.5840/jphil20009716.

Copeland, B. Jack, and Diane Proudfoot. "What Turing Did after He Invented the Universal Turing Machine." *Journal of Logic, Language and Information*, vol. 9, no. 4, 2000, pp. 491–509. *Springer Link*, doi:10.1023/A:1008371426608.

Crowley, Sharon. "Body Studies in Rhetoric and Composition." *Rhetoric and Composition as Intellectual Work*, edited by Gary A. Olson, Southern Illinois UP, 2002, pp. 177–87.

Dalyell, Tam. "Norman Routledge: Inspirational Teacher and Mathematician." *Independent*, 29 May, 2013, www.independent.co.uk/news/obituaries/norman-routledge-inspirational-teacher-and-mathematician-8635050.html.

David, Hugh. *On Queer Street: A Social History of British Homosexuality, 1895–1995*. HarperCollins, 1998.

Dolmage, Jay. "'Breathe upon Us an Even Flame': Hephaestus, History, and the Body of Rhetoric." *Rhetoric Review*, vol. 25, no. 2, 2006, pp. 119–40. *Taylor & Francis Online*, doi:10.1207/s15327981rr2502_1.

———. "Metis, *Mêtis, Mestiza*, Medusa: Rhetorical Bodies across Rhetorical Traditions." *Rhetoric Review*, vol. 28, no. 1, 2009, pp. 1–28. *Taylor & Francis Online*, doi:10.1080/07350190802540690.

Driskill, Qwo-Li. "Decolonial Skillshare: Indigenous Rhetorics as Radical Practice." *Survivance, Sovereignty, and Story: Teaching American Indian Rhetorics*, edited by Lisa King et al., Utah State UP, 2015, pp. 57–78.

———. "Doubleweaving Two-Spirit Critiques: Building Alliances between Native and Queer Studies." *GLQ: A Journal of Lesbian and Gay Studies*, vol. 16, no. 1–2, 2010, pp. 69–92. *Duke UP*, doi:10.1215/10642684-2009-013.

Easlea, Brian. *Fathering the Unthinkable: Masculinity, Scientists and the Nuclear Arms Race*. Pluto Press, 1987.

Edelman, Lee. *No Future: Queer Theory and the Death Drive.* Duke UP, 2004.

Edenfield, Avery C., et al. "Queering Tactical Technical Communication: DIY HRT." *Technical Communication Quarterly*, vol. 28, no. 3, 2019, pp. 177–91. *Taylor & Francis Online*, doi:10.1080/10572252.2019.1607906.

Edwell, Jennifer, et al. "Healing Arts: Rhetorical *Techne* as Medical (Humanities) Intervention." *Technical Communication Quarterly*, vol. 27, no. 1, 2018, pp. 50–63. *Taylor & Francis Online*, doi:10.1080/10572252.2018.1425960.

Fancher, Patricia. "Composing Artificial Intelligence: Performing Whiteness and Masculinity." *Present Tense: A Journal of Rhetoric in Society*, vol. 6, no. 1, 2016, https://www.presenttensejournal.org/volume-6/composing-artificial-intelligence/.

———. "My Body Is an Archive." *Catapult*, 10 Feb. 2020, catapult.co/stories/my-body-is-an-archive-essay-patricia-fancher.

Faris, Michael J. "Addressing Normativity in Technical Communication: Putting Technical Communication in Conversation with Queer Theory." *Conference for the Association of Teachers of Technical Communication*, Atlanta, GA, 2015.

———. "Queering Networked Writing: A Sensory Autoethnography of Desire and Sensation on Grindr." *Re/Orienting Writing Studies: Queer Methods, Queer Projects*, edited by William P. Banks et al., Utah State UP, 2019, pp. 127–49.

———. "Queer Kinesthetic Interlistening." *Peitho*, vol. 23, no. 1, 2020, cfshrc.org/article/queer-kinesthetic-interlistening/.

———. "Sex Education Comics: Feminist and Queer Approaches to Alternative Sex Education." *The Journal of Multimodal Rhetorics*, vol. 3, no. 1, 2019, journalofmultimodalrhetorics.com/3-1-issue-faris.

Fleckenstein, Kristie S. "Writing Bodies: Somatic Mind in Composition Studies." *College English*, vol. 61, no. 3, 1999, pp. 281–306. *JSTOR*, doi:10.2307/379070.

Foucault, Michel. "Friendship as a Way of Life." *Ethics: Subjectivity and Truth*, vol. 1. The New Press, 1997, pp. 135–40.

———. *The History of Sexuality, Volume 1: An Introduction.* Vintage Books, 1990.

Fountain, T. Kenny. *Rhetoric in the Flesh: Trained Vision, Technical Expertise, and the Gross Anatomy Lab.* Routledge, 2014.

Frost, Erin A. "Apparent Feminism as a Methodology for Technical Communication and Rhetoric." *Journal of Business and Technical Communication*, vol. 30, no. 1, 2015, pp. 3–28. *Sage Journals*, doi:10.1177/1050651915602295.

Gaboury, Jacob. "Darling Sweetheart: Queer Objects in Early Computer Art." *Virtual Creativity*, vol. 3, no. 1–2, 2013, pp. 23–27. *Intellect Discover*, doi: 10.1386/mvcr.3.1-2.23_1.

———. "On Uncomputable Numbers: The Origins of a Queer Computing." *NMC Media-N*, vol. 9, no. 2, 2013, median.newmediacaucus .org/caa-conference-edition-2013/on-uncomputable-numbers-the-origins-of-a-queer-computing/.

———. "A Queer History of Computing: Part One." *Rhizome*, Feb. 2013, rhizome.org/editorial/2013/feb/19/queer-computing-1/.

———. "A Queer History of Computing: Part Two." *Rhizome*, Mar. 2013, rhizome.org/editorial/2013/mar/19/queer-computing-2/.

———. "A Queer History of Computing: Part Three." *Rhizome*, Apr. 2013, rhizome.org/editorial/2013/apr/09/queer-history-computing-part-three/.

———. "A Queer History of Computing: Part Four." *Rhizome*, May 2013, rhizome.org/editorial/2013/may/06/queer-history-computing-part-four/.

———. "A Queer History of Computing, Part Five: Messages from the Unseen World." *Rhizome*, June 2013, rhizome.org/editorial/2013/jun/18/queer-history-computing-part-five/.

Gödel, Kurt. *On Formally Undecidable Propositions of Principia Mathematica and Related Systems*. Translated by B. Meltzer, Dover Publications, 1992.

Green, McKinley. "Resistance as Participation: Queer Theory's Applications for HIV Health Technology Design." *Technical Communication Quarterly*, vol. 30, no. 4, 2021, pp. 331–44. Taylor & Francis Online, doi:10.1080/10572252.2020.1831615.

———. "Risking Disclosure: Unruly Rhetorics and Queer(ing) HIV Risk Communication on Grindr." *Technical Communication Quarterly*, vol. 30, no.3, 2021, pp. 271–84. *Taylor & Francis Online*, doi:10.1080/10 572252.2021.1930185.

Grier, David Alan. "Human Computation and Divided Labor." *Handbook of Human Computation*, edited by Pietro Michelucci, Springer, Nov. 2013, pp. 13–23. *Springer Link*, doi:10.1007/978-1-4614-8806-4_3.

———. *When Computers Were Human*. Princeton UP, 2005.

Grint, Keith, and Rosalind Gill, editors. *The Gender-Technology Relation: Contemporary Theory and Research*. Taylor & Francis, 1995.

Grosz, Elizabeth. *Volatile Bodies: Toward a Corporeal Feminism*. Indiana UP, 1994.

Haas, Angela M. "Race, Rhetoric, and Technology: A Case Study of Decolonial Technical Communication Theory, Methodology, and

Pedagogy." *Journal of Business and Technical Communication*, vol. 26, no. 3, 2012, pp. 277–310. *ResearchGate*, doi:10.1177/1050651912439539.

———. "Wampum as Hypertext: An American Indian Intellectual Tradition of Multimedia Theory and Practice." *Studies in American Indian Literatures*, vol. 19, no. 4, 2007, pp. 77–100. *JSTOR*, jstor.org/stable/20737390.

Haas, Christina, and Stephen P. Witte. "Writing as an Embodied Practice: The Case of Engineering Standards." *Journal of Business and Technical Communication*, vol. 15, no. 4, 2001, pp. 413–57. *ResearchGate*, doi:10.1177/105065190101500402.

Haigh, Thomas. "Actually, Turing Did Not Invent the Computer." *Communications of the ACM*, vol. 57, no. 1, 2014, pp. 36–41. *ResearchGate*, doi:10.1145/2542504.

Halberstam, Judith. "Automating Gender: Postmodern Feminism in the Age of the Intelligent Machine." *Feminist Studies*, vol. 17, no. 3, 1991, pp. 439–60. *JSTOR*, doi:10.2307/3178281.

Haraway, Donna J. *Primate Visions: Gender, Race, and Nature in the World of Modern Science*. Routledge, 2013.

———. *Simians, Cyborgs, and Women: The Reinvention of Nature*. Routledge, 1990.

Hawkins, Ames. *These Are Love(d) Letters*. Wayne State UP, 2019.

Hayles, N. Katherine. *How We Became Posthuman: Virtual Bodies in Cybernetics, Literature, and Informatics*. U of Chicago P, 1999.

Hicks, Mar. *Programmed Inequality: How Britain Discarded Women Technologists and Lost Its Edge in Computing*. MIT Press, 2017.

Hodges, Andrew. *Alan Turing: The Enigma*. Simon & Schuster, 1983.

hooks, bell. "Are You Still a Slave? Liberating the Black Female Body." *The New School*, 2014, livestream.com/thenewschool/Slave?t=16231 71941.

———. "Eros, Eroticism and the Pedagogical Process." *Cultural Studies*, vol. 7, no. 1, 1993, pp. 58–63. *Taylor & Francis Online*, doi:10.1080/09502389300490051.

Isaacson, Walter. *The Innovators: How a Group of Hackers, Geniuses, and Geeks Created the Digital Revolution*. Simon & Schuster, 2014.

Itchuaqiyaq, Cana Uluak, and Breeanne Matheson. "Decolonizing Decoloniality: Considering the (Mis)Use of Decolonial Frameworks in TPC Scholarship." *Communication Design Quarterly*, vol. 9, no. 1, 2021, pp. 20–31. *ACM Digital Library*, doi:10.1145/3437000.3437002.

Jack, Jordynn. "Leviathan and the Breast Pump: Toward an Embodied Rhetoric of Wearable Technology." *Rhetoric Society Quarterly*, vol. 46, no. 3, 2016, pp. 207–21. *Raylor & Francis Online*, doi:10.1080/0277 3945.2016.1171691.

————. *Science on the Home Front: American Women Scientists in World War II.* U of Illinois P, 2009.

Jefferson, Geoffrey. "The Mind of Mechanical Man." *British Medical Journal,* vol. 1, no. 4616, 1949, pp. 1105–110. *JSTOR,* jstor.org/stable/25372573.

Johnson, Gavin. "(Queer) Optimism Ain't (Im)Possible." *The Routledge Handbook of Queer Rhetoric,* edited by Jaqueline Rhodes and Jonathan Alexander, Routledge, 2022, pp. 421–28.

Johnson, Maureen, et al. "Embodiment: Embodying Feminist Rhetorics." *Peitho,* vol. 18, no. 1, 2015. cfshrc.org/wp-content/uploads/2015/10/18.1Johnsonetal.pdf.

Jones, Natasha N., et al. "Disrupting the Past to Disrupt the Future: An Antenarrative of Technical Communication." *Technical Communication Quarterly,* vol. 25, no. 4, 2016, pp. 211–29. *Taylor & Francis Online,* doi:10.1080/10572252.2016.1224655.

Katz, Steven B. "The Ethic of Expediency: Classical Rhetoric, Technology, and the Holocaust." *College English,* vol. 54, no. 3, 1992, p. 255–75. *ResearchGate,* doi:10.2307/378062.

Keeling, Kara. "Queer OS." *Cinema Journal,* vol. 53, no. 2, 2014, pp. 152–57. *Project Muse,* doi:10.1353/cj.2014.0004.

Keller, Evelyn Fox. *Secrets of Life, Secrets of Death: Essays on Language, Gender, and Science.* Routledge, 1992.

King, Claire Sisko, and Isaac West. "This Could Be the Place: Queer Acceptance in *Lars and the Real Girl.*" *QED: A Journal in GLBTQ Worldmaking,* vol. 1, no. 3, 2014, pp. 59–84. *JSTOR,* doi:10.14321/qed.1.3.0059.

Kittler, Friedrich A. "There Is No Software." *Literature, Media, Information Systems: Essays,* edited by John Johnston, Routledge, 2013, pp. 147–55.

Kosma, Maria, and David R. Buchanan. "'Connect,' Log It, Track It, Go! *Techne*—Not Technology—and Embodiment to Achieve *Phronesis* in Exercise Promotion." *Quest,* vol. 70, no. 1, 2018, pp. 100–113. *Taylor & Francis Online,* doi:10.1080/00336297.2017.1355818.

Lassègue, Jean. "What Kind of Turing Test Did Turing Have in Mind?" *Tekhnema 3,* vol. Spring 1996.

Leavitt, David. *The Man Who Knew Too Much: Alan Turing and the Invention of the Computer.* W. W. Norton, 2006.

LeMesurier, Jennifer Lin. "Somatic Metaphors: Embodied Recognition of Rhetorical Opportunities." *Rhetoric Review,* vol. 33, no. 4, 2014, pp. 362–80. *Taylor & Francis Online,* doi:10.1080/07350198.2014.946868.

Link, David. "M.U.C. Love Letter Generator." Website. https://elmcip .net/node/1059.

Lloyd, Genevieve. *The Man of Reason: "Male" and "Female" in Western Philosophy*. 2nd ed., U of Minnesota P, 1993.

Lorde, Audre. "Poetry Is Not a Luxury." *The Selected Works of Audre Lorde*, edited by Roxane Gay, W. W. Norton, 2020, pp. 3–8.

———. "Uses of the Erotic: The Erotic as Power." *The Selected Works of Audre Lorde*, edited by Roxane Gay, W. W. Norton, 2020, pp. 29–38.

Love, Heather. *Feeling Backward: Loss and the Politics of Queer History*. Harvard UP, 2009.

McPherson, Tara. "U.S. Operating Systems at Mid-Century: The Intertwining of Race and UNIX." *Race after the Internet*, edited by Lisa Nakamura and Peter Chow-White, Routledge, 2011, pp. 27–43.

Medina-López, Kelly. "Rasquache Rhetorics: A Cultural Rhetorics Sensibility." *Constellations: A Cultural Rhetorics Publishing Space*, vol. 1, no. 1, 2018, pp. 1–20.

Melonçon, Lisa. "Bringing the Body Back through Performative Phenomenology." *Methodologies for the Rhetoric of Health and Medicine*, edited by Lisa Meloncon and J. Blake Scott, Routledge, 2017, pp. 96–114.

———. "Embodied Personas for a Mobile World." *Technical Communication*, vol. 64, no. 1, Feb. 2017, pp. 50–65.

———. "Toward a Theory of Technological Embodiment." *Rhetorical Accessibility: At the Intersection of Technical Communication and Disability Studies*, Routledge, 2013, pp. 67–81.

Milbourne, Chelsea Redeker, and Sarah Hallenbeck. "Gender, Material Chronotopes, and the Emergence of the Eighteenth-Century Microscope." *Rhetoric Society Quarterly*, vol. 43, no. 5, 2013, pp. 401–24. Taylor & Francis Online, doi:10.1080/02773945.2013.828096.

Moore, Kristen R., and Daniel P. Richards, editors. *Posthuman Praxis in Technical Communication*. Routledge, 2018.

Morris, Charles E., III, and K. J. Rawson. "Queer Archives/Archival Queers." *Theorizing Histories of Rhetoric*, edited by Michelle Ballif, Southern Illinois UP, 2013, pp. 74–89.

Morrison, Margaret. "Laughing with Queers in My Eyes: Proposing 'Queer Rhetoric(s)' and Introducing a Queer Issue." *Pre/Text: A Journal of Rhetorical Theory*, vol. 13, no. 3–4, 1992, pp. 11–36.

Moschovakis, Yiannis, and Mike Yates. "In Memoriam: Robin Oliver Gandy 1919–1995." *Bulletin of Symbolic Logic*, vol. 2, no. 3, 1996, pp. 367–70. Cambridge UP, doi:10.1017/S1079898600007873.

Muñoz, José Esteban. *Cruising Utopia: The Then and There of Queer Futurity*. New York UP, 2009.

Noble, Safiya Umoja. *Algorithms of Oppression: How Search Engines Reinforce Racism*. New York UP, 2018.

"Norman Routledge - Being Friends with Alan Turing (60/139)." *YouTube*, uploaded by *Web of Stories: Life Stories of Remarkable People*, 10 July 2017, www.youtube.com/watch?v=lTVWKYLjSOU&list=PLVV0r6CmEsFy0scpmp2JOe87muCf5O1dg&index=61.

"Norman Routledge - Glad to Be Gay (72/139)" *YouTube*, uploaded by *Web of Stories: Life Stories of Remarkable People*, 10 July 2017, youtube.com/watch?v=eVR7yPwZGu8&list=PLVV0r6CmEsFy0scpmp2JOe87muCf5O1dg&index=72.

"Norman Routledge - Something Alan Turing Told Me about Homosexuality (66/139)" *YouTube*, uploaded by *Web of Stories: Life Stories of Remarkable People*, 10 July 2017, youtube.com/watch?v=7Qh0dRTCK8s&list=PLVV0r6CmEsFy0scpmp2JOe87muCf5O1dg&index=66.

Oleksiak, Timothy. "Queering Rhetorical Listening: An Introduction to a Cluster Conversation." *Peitho*, vol. 23, no. 1, 2020, cfshrc.org/article/queering-rhetorical-listening-an-introduction-to-a-cluster-conversation/.

Pender, Kelly. *Techne, from Neoclassicism to Postmodernism: Understanding Writing as a Useful, Teachable Art*. Parlor Press, 2011.

Petersdorff, Ann von. "Embodied Encounters: A Case for Autobiographical and Haptic Filmmaking." *Constellations: A Cultural Rhetorics Publishing Space*, vol. 1, no. 1, 2018.

Pritchard, Eric Darnell. *Fashioning Lives: Black Queers and the Politics of Literacy*. Southern Illinois UP, 2017.

Rawson, K. J. "Accessing Transgender // Desiring Queer(Er?) Archival Logics." *Archivaria*, vol. 68, 2009, pp. 123–40.

———. "The Rhetorical Power of Archival Description: Classifying Images of Gender Transgression." *Rhetoric Society Quarterly*, vol. 48, no. 4, 2018, pp. 327–51. *Taylor & Francis Online,* doi:10.1080/02773945.2017.1347951.

———. "Transgender Worldmaking in Cyberspace: Historical Activism on the Internet." *QED: A Journal in GLBTQ Worldmaking*, vol. 1, no. 2, 2014, pp. 38–60. *JSTOR*, doi:10.14321/qed.1.2.0038.

Rees, Mina. "Mathematical Sciences and WWII." *The American Mathematical Monthly*, vol. 87, no. 8, 1980, pp. 607–21. *Taylor & Francis Online*, tandfonline.com/doi/abs/10.1080/00029890.1980.1199510.

Reyes, G. Mitchell. "Stranger Relations: The Case for Rebuilding Commonplaces between Rhetoric and Mathematics." *Rhetoric Society Quarterly*, vol. 44, no. 5, 2014, pp. 470–91. *Taylor & Francis Online*, doi:10.1080/02773945.2014.965046.

Rhodes, Jacqueline, and Jonathan Alexander. "Introduction." *Routledge Handbook of Queer Rhetoric*, edited by Jacqueline Rhodes and Jonathan Alexander, Routledge, 2022, pp. 1–4.

———. *Techne: Queer Meditations on Writing the Self*. Computers and Composition Digital Press/Utah State UP, 2015, ccdigitalpress.org/techne.

Ríos, Gabriela Raquel. "Cultivating Land-Based Literacies and Rhetorics." *Literacy in Composition Studies*, vol. 3, no. 1, 2015, pp. 60–70. *LiCS*, doi:10.21623/1.3.1.5.

———. "Performing Nahua Rhetorics for Civic Engagement." *Survivance, Sovereignty, and Story: Teaching American Indian Rhetorics*, edited by Lisa King et al., Utah State UP, 2015, pp. 79–95.

Roberts, Siobhan. "Christopher Strachey's Nineteen-Fifties Love Machine." *The New Yorker*, 14 Feb. 2017, www.newyorker.com/tech/annals-of-technology/christopher-stracheys-nineteen-fifties-love-machine.

Rose, Emma J., and Rebecca Walton. "Factors to Actors: Implications of Posthumanism for Social Justice Work." *Posthuman Praxis in Technical Communication*, edited by Kristen R. Moore and Daniel P. Richards, Routledge, 2018. pp. 1–10, Doi.org/10.1145/2775441.2775464.

Royster, Jacqueline Jones, and Gesa E. Kirsch. *Feminist Rhetorical Practices: New Horizons for Rhetoric, Composition, and Literacy Studies*. Southern Illinois UP, 2012.

Rumens, Nick. *Queer Company: The Role and Meaning of Friendship in Gay Men's Work Lives*. Routledge, 2016.

Sauer, Beverly. *The Rhetoric of Risk: Technical Documentation in Hazardous Environments*. Routledge, 2002.

Schell, Eileen E., and K. J. Rawson, editors. *Rhetorica in Motion: Feminist Rhetorical Methods and Methodologies*. U of Pittsburgh P, 2010.

Schnelle, Helmut. "A Note on Enjoying Strawberries with Cream, Making Mistakes, and Other Idiotic Features." *Alan Turing: Life and Legacy of a Great Thinker*, edited by Christof Teuscher, Springer Berlin Heidelberg, 2004, pp. 353–58.

Schryer, Catherine F., et al. "Technē or Artful Science and the Genre of Case Presentations in Healthcare Settings." *Communication Monographs*, vol. 72, no. 2, 2005, pp. 234–60. *Taylor & Francis Online*, doi:10.1080/03637750500120485.

Sedgwick, Eve Kosofsky. *Epistemology of the Closet*. Updated ed., U of California P, 2008.

———. "Paranoid Reading and Reparative Reading, or, You're so Paranoid, You Probably Think This Essay Is about You." *Touching Feeling: Affect, Pedagogy, Performativity*, Duke UP, 2003, pp. 123–52.

Seidler, Victor Jeleniewski. *Man Enough: Embodying Masculinities*. SAGE Publications, 1997.

Selzer, Jack, and Sharon Crowley, editors. *Rhetorical Bodies*. U of Wisconsin P, 1999.

Serlin, David. *Replaceable You: Engineering the Body in Postwar America*. U of Chicago P, 2004.

Shelton, Cecilia D. *On Edge: A Techné of Marginality*. East Carolina U, 2019, PhD Dissertation.

Smilges, J. Logan. *Queer Silence: On Disability and Rhetorical Absence*. U of Minnesota P, 2022.

Strachey, Christopher. "M.U.C Love Letter Generator." Computer Program, 1952.

———. "The 'Thinking' Machine." *Encounter*, October 1954, pp. 25–31.

Swinton, Jonathan. *Alan Turing's Manchester*. Infang Publishing, 2019.

Teston, Christa. *Bodies in Flux: Scientific Methods for Negotiating Medical Uncertainty*. U of Chicago P, 2017.

Tran, Jess, and Elizabeth Patitsas. "The Computer as a Queer Object." *SocArXiv*, 4 Dec. 2020. *SOCARXIV Papers*, doi:10.31235/osf.io/afuqs.

Turing, Alan. "Can Automatic Calculating Machines Be Said to Think? (1952)" *The Essential Turing*, edited by B. Jack Copeland, Oxford UP, 2004, pp. 476–86.

———. "Computing Machinery and Intelligence (1950)." *The Essential Turing*, edited by B. Jack Copeland, Oxford UP, 2004, pp. 433–64.

———. "Intelligent Machinery (1948)." *The Essential Turing*, edited by B. Jack Copeland, Oxford UP, 2004, pp. 395–432.

———. "On Computable Numbers, with an Application to the Entscheidungsproblem (1938)." *The Essential Turing*, edited by B. Jack Copeland, Oxford UP, 2004, pp. 58–90.

VanHaitsma, Pamela. "Gossip as Rhetorical Methodology for Queer and Feminist Historiography." *Rhetoric Review*, vol. 35, no. 2, 2016, pp. 135–47. *Taylor & Francis Online*, doi:10.1080/07350198.2016.1142845.

———. *Queering Romantic Engagement in the Postal Age: A Rhetorical Education*. U of South Carolina P, 2019.

———. "What Can *The Favourite* Tell Us about the Rhetoric of Queer Letters?" *Citizen Critics*, 22 Feb. 2019.

Waite, Stacey. "How (and Why) to Write Queer: A Failing, Impossible, Contradictory Instruction Manual for Scholars of Writing Studies." *Re/Orienting Writing Studies: Queer Methods, Queer Projects*, edited by William P. Banks et al., Utah State UP, 2019, pp. 42–54.

Walker, Harron. "The Moment I Stopped Knowing How to Label My Sexuality." *W* Magazine, 16 Feb. 2021, www.wmagazine.com/life/harron-walker-sexuality-column.

Walton, Rebecca, and Godwin Y. Agboka, editors. *Equipping Technical Communicators for Social Justice Work: Theories, Methodologies, and Pedagogies.* Utah State UP, 2021.

Whitby, Blay. *Artificial Intelligence.* Rosen Publishing Group, 2009.

Wickman, Chad. "Rhetoric, *Technê*, and the Art of Scientific Inquiry." *Rhetoric Review*, vol. 31, no. 1, 2012, pp. 21–40. *Taylor & Francis Online*, doi:10.1080/07350198.2012.630953.

Wiener, Norbert. *The Human Use of Human Beings: Cybernetics and Society.* Da Capo Press, 1954.

"write a love letter." ChatGPT, version GPT-3.5, OpenAI, 14 Oct. 2023, chat.openai.com/chat.

"write a love letter from a man to another man." ChatGPT, version GPT-3.5, OpenAI, 14 Oct. 2023, chat.openai.com/chat.

ARCHIVAL SOURCES

National Archives for the History of Computing Collection, Manchester University Library

"Ferranti Mark I Log Books, 1951." Box 6, vol. 1, GB 133 NAHC/ MUC/2/C6, University of Manchester Department of Computer Science Collection. National Archive for the History of Computing, University of Manchester Library, Manchester, UK. Accessed July 6, 2016. https://archiveshub.jisc.ac.uk/manchesteruniversity/data/ gb133-nahc/muc/nahc/muc/2/c.

"Ferranti Mark I Log Books, 1952." Box 6, vol. 2, GB 133 NAHC/ MUC/2/C6, University of Manchester Department of Computer Science Collection. National Archive for the History of Computing, University of Manchester Library, Manchester, UK. Accessed July 6, 2016. https://archiveshub.jisc.ac.uk/manchesteruniversity/data/ gb133-nahc/muc/nahc/muc/2/c.

"Summary of Work in Progress on the Manchester University Electronic Computer Mk II, October 1952." Box 11, folder A, GB 133 NAHC/ MUC/2/C11(a), University of Manchester Department of Computer Science Collection. National Archive for the History of Computing, University of Manchester Library, Manchester, UK. Accessed July 5, 2016. https://archiveshub.jisc.ac.uk/manchesteruniversity/data/ gb133-nahc/muc/nahc/muc/2/c.

"Ferranti Mark I Log Books, 1953." Box 6, vol. 3, GB 133 NAHC/ MUC/2/C6, University of Manchester Department of Computer Science Collection. National Archive for the History of Computing, University of Manchester Library, Manchester, UK. Accessed July 6, 2016. https://archiveshub.jisc.ac.uk/manchesteruniversity/data/ gb133-nahc/muc/nahc/muc/2/c.

"Ferranti I Log Books, 1954." Box 6, vol. 4, GB 133 NAHC/MUC/2/ C6, University of Manchester Department of Computer Science Collection. National Archive for the History of Computing, University of Manchester Library, Manchester, UK. Accessed July 6, 2016. https://

archiveshub.jisc.ac.uk/manchesteruniversity/data/gb133-nahc/muc/
nahc/muc/2/c

"Ferranti Mark I Log Books, 1958." Box 6, vol. 6, GB 133 NAHC/
MUC/2/C6, University of Manchester Department of Computer
Science Collection. National Archive for the History of Computing,
University of Manchester Library, Manchester, UK. Accessed July
6, 2016. https://archiveshub.jisc.ac.uk/manchesteruniversity/data/
gb133-nahc/muc/nahc/muc/2/c.

"Mercury Programming Library, c 1958–62." Box 17, vol. 1–4, GB
133 NAHC/MUC/2/C17, University of Manchester Department of
Computer Science Collection. National Archive for the History of
Computing, University of Manchester Library, Manchester, UK. Accessed July 6, 2016. https://archiveshub.jisc.ac.uk/manchesteruniver-
sity/data/gb133-nahc/muc/nahc/muc/2/c.

"Correspondence with users of Mercury, Nottingham University." Box 2,
folder 7, GB 133 NAHC/MUC/2/B7, University of Manchester Department of Computer Science Collection. National Archive for the
History of Computing, University of Manchester Library, Manchester,
UK. Accessed July 6, 2016. https://archiveshub.jisc.ac.uk/manchester
university/data/gb133-nahc/muc/nahc/muc/2/b.

"Miscellaneous correspondence, c 1958–62." Box 5, folder C, GB 133
NAHC/MUC/2/B5c, University of Manchester Department of
Computer Science Collection. National Archive for the History of
Computing, University of Manchester Library, Manchester, UK.
Accessed July 6, 2016. https://archiveshub.jisc.ac.uk/manchesterunive
rsity/data/gb133-nahc/muc/nahc/muc/2/b.

Alan Turing Digital Archive

Strachey, Christopher. Letter to Alan Turing, 15 May 1951. Box D, folder
5, AMT/D 5: image 3a–d, Turing Digital Archive, Turing papers held
in the Archive Centre at King's College, Cambridge.

Gandy, Robin. Letter to Alan Turing, circa 1951. Box D, folder 15,
AMT/D/15. 2: image 2–2e, Turing Digital Archive, Accessed Online.
Turing papers held in the Archive Centre at King's College, Cambridge.

Routledge, Norman. Letter to Alan Turing, circa 1952. Box D, folder
5, AMT/D/5: image 14a–c, Turing Digital Archive, Accessed Online.
Turing papers held in the Archive Centre at King's College, Cambridge.

Turing, Alan. Letter to Norman Routledge circa Feb 1952. Box D, folder
14a, AMT/D 14a: image 1 and 1A, Turing Digital Archive, Accessed
Online. Turing papers held in the Archive Centre at King's College,
Cambridge.

Image Sources

Figure 1: "Manchester Mark I computer, 1948." University of Manchester Department of Computer Science Collection, John Rylands Research Institute and Library, March 2022, https://rylandscollections.com/2023/06/21/a-new-view-of-the-manchester-computer/. Copyright of the University of Manchester.

Figure 2: "Manchester Mark I engineer's log, December 24, 1958." Box 2, folder C6, nach/mac/2/c6, University of Manchester Department of Computer Science Collection. National Archive for the History of Computing, University of Manchester Library, Manchester, UK. Copyright of the University of Manchester. http://archiveshub.jisc.ac.uk/manchesteruniversity/data/gb133-nahc/muc/nahc/muc/2/c6.

Figure 3: "Photograph of Alan Turing running." Box D, folder 15, AMT/D/15. 2: image 2–2e, Turing Digital Archive, Accessed Online. Photograph held in the Archive Centre at King's College, Cambridge. https://turingarchive.kings.cam.ac.uk/material-given-kings-college-cambridge-1960-amtk/amt-k-7-8.

Figure 4: Photograph of Manchester Mark I with labeled components published in *The Illustrated London News*, June 25, 1949." Box D, folder 2, GB 133 NAHC/MUC/D2 University of Manchester Department of Computer Science Collection. National Archive for the History of Computing, University of Manchester Library, Manchester, UK. https://archiveshub.jisc.ac.uk/manchesteruniversity/archives/ed856179-56d0-31b6-97a4-c4b10a9055a1?terms=London%20Times&component=6f56f7c4-481a-36a1-9b34-1a809d910cfb.

Figure 5: "Love letter by Christopher Strachey's program." Photograph by Nicole McCormick, September 30, 2012. https://www.flickr.com/photos/ohhgroovy/8037582535/in/photolist-2nnCgsn-dffHge-2nuNvNY-6oAog1-FbX5Cg/.

Figure 6: "Section from Christopher Strachey's article 'The Thinking Machine.'" *Encounter*, October 1954, pp. 25–31.

Figure 7: "Letter from Alan Turing to Norman Routledge, February 1952." The Turing Digital Archive, AMT/D/14a page 2. https://turingarchive.kings.cam.ac.uk/correspondence-amtd/amt-d-14a.

Figure 8: "Unidentified Woman operating the Ferranti Mark I computer, 1953." Computer History Museum Collection, Item id: 102645389. https://www.computerhistory.org/chess/stl-430b9bbe6b611/.

Figure 9: "Logbook entry from August 12, 1953, signed "operated by Miss Ward" from midnight until 8:00 a.m." Box 6, vol. 3, GB 133 NAHC/MUC/2/C6, Ferranti Mark I Log Books, University of Manchester Department of Computer Science Collection. National Archive for the

History of Computing, University of Manchester Library, Manchester, UK. Copyright of the University of Manchester.

Figure 10: "Two entries signed by M. Audrey Bates on Sunday, August 26, 1953." Box 6, vol. 3, GB 133 NAHC/MUC/2/C6, Ferranti Mark I Log Books, University of Manchester Department of Computer Science Collection. National Archive for the History of Computing, University of Manchester Library, Manchester, UK. Copyright of the University of Manchester.

INDEX

The letter p following a page locator denotes a photograph.

AUTHOR

Patricia Fancher has a PhD in rhetoric and studies rhetorical theory, feminist and queer rhetoric, and digital media. She teaches courses on feminist writing, digital storytelling, rhetoric, and creative nonfiction. Her research has been published in *Peitho, Composition Studies, Rhetoric Review, Present Tense, Computers & Composition*, and *Enculturation*. In addition to her scholarly work, Fancher is a creative writer, with essays about feminism and sexuality on many mainstream and literary platforms, including *The Washington Post, Huffington Post, The Sun, Autostraddle*, and *Catapult*. She lives in Santa Barbara, California, with her two cats, who are her most loyal writing buddies.

Photo credit: Ian King of Santa Barbara, CA

BOOKS IN THE CCCC STUDIES IN WRITING & RHETORIC SERIES

This book was typeset in Adobe Garamond and Frutiger by
Barbara Frazier.
Typefaces used on the cover include Garamond and New Gothic Std.
The book was printed on 50-lb. White Offset paper.